Excel

YEAR 7

English Workbook

ESSENTIAL skills

Get the Results You Want!

PASCAL PRESS

Jane Baker

Reprinted 2001, 2002, 2003, 2004, 2005, 2006, 2008 (twice), 2010, 2011

Updated in 2012 for the Australian Curriculum

Reprinted 2014, 2015, 2016, 2017 (twice), 2019, 2020, 2021, 2022, 2023, 2024, 2025

ISBN 978 1 74020 036 3

Pascal Press
PO Box 250
Glebe NSW 2037
www.pascalpress.com.au

Publisher: Vivienne Joannou
Project editor: Mark Dixon
Edited by Valerie Marlborough and Frances Wade
Typeset by The Type Group and Grizzly Graphics (Leanne Richters)
Cover by DiZign Pty Ltd
Printed by Vivar Printing/Green Giant Press

CONTENTS

Index of punctuation and grammar content

Chapter	Punctuation	Grammar
1 Cartoon	Capital letters and full stops	Sentence (subject and predicate)
2 Diary entry	Full stops and abbreviations	Compound sentences and coordinate conjunctions (two equally important ideas joined by *and* or *but*)
3 Personal letter	Revision (full stops and capitals)	Complex sentences and subordinate conjunctions
4 Factual recount	Question and exclamation marks	Questions and exclamations
5 Narrative	Commas (separating list items; separating activities)	Verbs: being and doing words
6 Interview	Commas (separating complete ideas; separating words and their explanation)	Verbs and tenses (times)
7 Play script	Inverted commas (for direct speech)	Verbs (continuous tenses)
8 Book jacket	Inverted commas (titles; quotations)	Verbs (future tense forms)
9 Instruction	Apostrophe of abbreviation	Verb and subject agreement
10 Factual description	Apostrophe of possession	Adjectives and adjectival phrases
11 Advertisement	Apostrophe of possession with uncommon plurals	Adjectives: comparative and superlative forms
12 Sports article	Hyphens (as word breaks and word links)	Personal pronouns
13 Song lyric	Colons (indicating direct speech follows; introducing a list or explanation)	Relative pronouns
14 Poem	Colons and commas	Adverbs of manner and degree
15 Television review	Revision (all punctuation)	Adverbs of time and place

To the student

This book is designed to help you master the basic skills of writing and understanding English. It will help you follow work you are doing in class by providing clear text commentaries on all the different kinds of writing you are required to do at school.

The work in each chapter develops in stages from Chapter 1 to Chapter 15. As you work through the chapters you will find you are managing harder work without difficulty.

To use this book you will need the assistance of a good dictionary. A Macquarie, an Oxford or a Collins dictionary will be the most helpful.

Carefully examine the examples at the beginning of each exercise before you begin writing. These will show you how to do the exercise. Learn any rules that apply to the exercises so that you can use them when you write in class.

Read the questions carefully before writing so that you answer exactly what is asked. In multiple-choice questions choose the most accurate answer. Some may be possible answers but there will always be one that is the best answer.

When you approach the writing tasks at the end of each chapter try to use what you have learned in that chapter to help you write a good paragraph or whole text.

Your use of this book means you want to improve your writing skills. If you use it carefully, your writing will certainly improve.

Good luck!

Jane Baker

CHAPTER 1

Cartoon

STRUCTURE

Strip

Frame 1 — **introduction**
- *text sets story base*
- *illustration sets scene*

Frame 2 / **Frame 3** — **body of story**
- *Wal's decision*
- *Wal's ride*

Frame 4 — **conclusion**
- *relief: the dog 'made it'*

LANGUAGE FEATURES

1. brevity
2. simplicity
3. conciseness

onomatopoeic *(sound) words suggest energy and action*

simple sentence sets story in motion

- *short exclamatory sentences suggest confident decicion*
- ***colloquial*** *(everyday) expression establishes close relationship of Wal and The Dog*

single word as exclamation suggests explosion of speed

- *two phrases: suggesting heartfelt thanks and relief contrast with the confidence of complete sentences in frames 1 and 2*
- *contrast with confidence of complete sentences in frames 1 and 2*

Comprehension

(Note: These cartoon characters, known as Wal and The Dog, are the main subjects of Murray Ball's *Footrot Flats* books.)

1 Wal has always been sure he could leap the drain on his bike. Is this true or false? ____________________

2 Underline the correct answer. *Hang on to your hat* suggests the bike jump will be:

a dangerous **b** fast **c** destructive of clothing

3 What is Wal's fate? ____________________

____

4 The Dog's response to the jump is:

a elation **b** exhaustion **c** relief **d** apathy

5 Compare the texts in frames 1 and 4. Whose story is really being told in this cartoon?

____

Writing skills

1 Insert the missing letters. Cartoons tell a story in t _ _ t and i l l _ s t _ _ tion.

2 Underline all correct answers. The text of a cartoon is:

a concise **b** very detailed **c** brief **d** simple **e** always very funny

3 Frame 1 contains two pieces of text. One piece suggests uncertainty and the other certainty.

Which suggests which? ____

4 Insert the missing letters. Frame 1 sets the sc _ n _ for the story, frames 2 and 3 tell the s _ _ _ y and frame 4 provides the con _ _ _ _ ion.

5 Underline the correct answer. The extra letters R in the word *GROOM* in frame 1 suggest:

a bad temper **b** a revved motor **c** an attempt to add more text

6 Insert the missing letters. Frame 2 is drawn in close-up to allow us to see the contrasting exp _ _ _ _ ions on the faces of Wal and The Dog.

7 How do both text and illustration in frame 3 suggest power and speed? ______________________

____

____

8 Underline the correct answer. The punchline of this cartoon lies in:

a the picture of Wal's crash **b** The Dog's comment at the end

9 Underline the correct answer. The humour of this cartoon lies in:

a Wal's accident **b** Wal's showing-off

c the sharp drawing of facial expressions **d** The Dog's survival and his comment

10 Underline the correct answer. The tone of this cartoon is:

a cruel **b** mean **c** light **d** serious

Vocabulary

illustration	**diagram**	**caricature**	**portrait**	**frame**
text	**dialogue**	**cartoonist**	**commentator**	**humorous**

Each word in the vocabulary list relates to the text type of this chapter. Check that you know what the words mean, using a good dictionary. Then learn to spell them, using the Look, Cover, Write, Check method.

Look: Study the word closely, paying special attention to the difficult parts.

Cover: Cover the word and try to see it in your mind's eye.

Write: Write the word without looking back.

Check: Check your spelling. If it is not correct, repeat the process.

Focus on punctuation

Capital letters and full stops

Capital letters begin:
- sentences
- proper nouns
- titles

1 Add capital letters,

e.g. *ring dr smith for an appointment.*
Ring Dr Smith for an appointment.

a when the principal, mrs taylor, arrives, tell her mrs jones called.

b even though he is twenty, peter does not have a driving licence.

c feroza's meats is an excellent butcher shop.

d john's father runs a carpentry workshop called woodchips.

e although brompton high school faces lyons road its entry is on miller street.

Full stops:
- end sentences
- mark most abbreviations, e.g. *Capt.* for *Captain*, *Feb.* for *February*

2 Add full stops,

e.g. *Bryson and Co are a legal firm.*
Bryson and Co. are a legal firm.

a James Jones travelled to Cairns

b Rev John Hales conducted a service

c Maj Henry Lewis is in charge of supplies

d The Hon John Howard is a former prime minister of Australia

e The South Seas Fishing Coop has gone bankrupt

Select a word

From the vocabulary list choose words that mean the same as the following.

1 a true picture of a person ______________________

2 a drawing ______________________

3 funny______________________

4 a plan ______________________

5 a piece of writing ______________________

6 an actor's words in a play ______________________

Grammar

Sentences, common nouns and proper nouns

A **sentence** contains one complete idea. It has a subject and a predicate, e.g.
John ran to school. = a sentence
Subject Predicate

The subject is the person or thing that the predicate tells us about.

1 Indicate the subject with a single underline and the predicate with a double underline.

a Judy Horacek and Cathy Wilcox are well-known Australian cartoonists.

b Michael Leunig, the Victorian cartoonist, has had several books published.

c Larson is a much-loved American cartoonist.

d Some cartoonists go on to make animated films like *Happy Feet*.

e Some films about an animated character are set in the real world.

Any group of words that does not have a subject and a predicate is called a fragment, e.g.
a green tree, is falling, under the bed = three fragments

2 Write S (Sentence) or F (Fragment) after each of these.

a the moon _____
b Clouds passed over the moon _____
c Peter caught a shining fish _____
d a shining fish _____
e as evening fell _____
f a swarm of very angry bees _____
g A sleek lizard twitched its tail lazily _____

- **Nouns** are the names of people, places and things.
- **Common nouns** are general names, e.g. *boy, girl, country*.
- Common nouns are concrete or abstract, e.g.
  table, chair, water, wood, silk = concrete nouns
  happiness, anxiety, fear, elasticity, density = abstract nouns
- **Proper nouns** are special names, e.g. *Paul, Maria, Australia.*

3 Indicate the common nouns with a single underline and the proper nouns with a double underline, e.g. *Tony Yu and Peter Chin play tennis which they learned as children in Hong Kong.*

a Ginger Meggs is one of Australia's oldest cartoon characters.

b Cartoons of former prime minister, Paul Keating, often presented him as an undertaker.

c Caricatures always exaggerate our obvious features, e.g. bushy eyebrows.

d Animators have given us the Road Runner, Bugs Bunny and Mickey Mouse.

e Political cartoonists suggest ideas in their sketches and do not fill in every detail.

4 Write 'abstract' or 'concrete' to describe the underlined common nouns.

a Cartoonists rely on humour to engage the reader. ____________________

b Fear and anxiety were written on her face. **i** ____________________ **ii** ____________________

c The waves crashed on to the beach. ____________________

d Dogs like company and friendship. **i** ____________________ **ii** ____________________

Word study

1 Insert a word from the vocabulary list into each of the following:

a Most cartoons are ____________________ rather than serious.

b A ____________________ tells his story in pictures and ____________________.

c Each section of a strip cartoon is called a ____________________.

d A cartoonist's picture of someone is not a true ____________________ but a ____________________.

e A ______________ shows how something works but an ______________ shows appearance and emotions.

f A football ____________________________ must know the rules to be able to comment fairly.

2 Find words in the vocabulary list that mean the same as the following.

a a drawing showing the outline of an object and its parts ____________________

b one who writes and talks in the media about current events ____________________

c a conversation between two people ____________________

d a picture to demonstrate a point ____________________

Word usage

Fire guts heritage building

O'Connelltown, Thursday

Fire brigades fought for five hours to control a major blaze in Todman Street last night.

Believed to have started in the exhaust flue of the adjacent chicken shop, the fire quickly took hold of the old Oriental Bank building. Its ancient dried timbers and fibrous plaster were well alight by the time the town brigade arrived.

Despite reinforcements from surrounding areas firemen were unable to quench the flames. About 9 pm the handsome facade of the old building collapsed outward into the street burying several parked cars.

By morning only the smoking remains of a couple of external walls were left. These will have to be demolished as they have been rendered unstable by the fierce heat.

1 Match these to underlined words in the passage.

a additional help ____________________ **b** struggled ____________________

c next door ____________________ **d** extinguish ____________________

e very old ____________________ **f** outside ____________________

2 Underline the correct answer.

a Fibrous plaster contains:

i horsehair **ii** bluemetal **iii** nails **iv** bleach

b 'Handsome' in the words *handsome facade* means:

i pretty **ii** well-painted **iii** decorated **iv** impressive

3 Select an underlined word from the passage to fill in the blanks.

a The ____________________ castle was still sound after 600 years.

b John's house of cards ____________________ in a heap.

c The ____________________ of the meal were put in the fridge.

4 Find words in the text to match these meanings:

a significant ____________________ **b** organised group ____________________

c relics ____________________ **d** outside ____________________

Quick think

Match the people listed in Column A with the words from the vocabulary list in Column B.

Column A	**Column B**
1 cartoonist	**a** dialogue
2 illustrator	**b** caricature
3 actor	**c** portrait
4 artist	**d** diagram
5 draftsperson	**e** illustration

Proofreading

Insert missing punctuation and correct misspelt words in the passage.

All majer newspapers cary cartunes of too knds, humerous and social coment Each paper has its owne cartoonists who prodyuce their cartoons about currant issues, e.g. cathy wilcox whose cartoons appear in the *sydney mcrning herald* sometimes poeple are offended by the way a cartounist has shone them and in this case they may ask a lawer for help however, most people take cartoons in a spirit of fun

Idiom

Explain:

1 For John, the grass was always greener over the hill.

2 Sally wailed, 'It never rains but it pours.'

Writing paragraphs and whole texts

1 Create the text for this cartoon.

(Hint: Think about the routine of a dog's life and the routine of the family who owns him.)

2 In your own words explain what issue Kudelka is highlighting in this cartoon. In your answer consider what message the text gives us and how the image of the cow helps to enhance that message. Make sure you tell us who might not be negotiating and why.

Greenhouse Policy:
We do not negotiate
with flatulent cows.

3 **a** Draw your own cartoon. It can be a humorous one with two or three frames or a serious one with a message about an important issue like water conservation or bushfire protection.

b Explain what your cartoon is saying in three or four correctly punctuated sentences.

4 Write a brief explanation of why you would or would not like to be a cartoonist or an animator when you finish school. Use words like *career, profession, satisfaction, skills, opportunity, training, experience, preference.*

Chapter test

1 Which is a complete sentence?

a Under the table asleep.

b The cat under the table asleep.

c The white cat under the table asleep.

d The white cat under the table is asleep.

2 Which sentence is correctly punctuated?

a mr harris is a fisherman

b Mr Harris is a fisherman

c Mr Harris is a fisherman.

d Mr. Harris is a fisherman.

CHAPTER 2

Diary entry

STRUCTURE

date entry is written

introduction:
- *introduces main idea of whole diary entry—the problem with Ed*
- *includes lead-in sentence to start the topic—Ed*

James's bad afternoon with Ed has several parts; each part has a separate paragraph

each paragraph follows the development of James's bad afternoon in ***sequence*** *(order of its happening)*

body of text

conclusion: *sums up what James feels about Ed and the sort of a day he's had*

October 12

Ed, Ed. Save me from Ed! I came home from school today and I could tell, in one way or another, I was going to be in trouble. She was just in one of those moods. One of those strung out 'I'm going to have a complete and utter breakdown,' moods.

So I sit here at my desk hoping she'll forget I exist. No, the door slams open, Ed looms. 'Right!' she says 'Did you put them back in here dirty?' I shook my head. I could tell she was trying to make me argue with her so she could scream back at me. I watched her pick up each sock and give it a hearty sniff. 'They smell!' she announced.

Then she picked up a pair of underwear and gave that a good sniff. I just hoped they were clean, for her sake. 'You know what this smells of?' I shook my head. 'Cat!' The most dreaded word in her vocabulary. Then she peered more closely at it. Shocked and amazed she plucked off a tiny hair, which she shortly foisted under my nose. 'It's not hygienic!' she shrieked.

I told her that I don't mind if Vicious sleeps in there. Little blasts of steam were coming out of her ears by then. 'That cat is sleeping outside from now on!' She pointed a trembling finger at me and turned red. Then she took just about every piece of clothing I've ever worn, except maybe some blue booties in the bottom of the drawer, and marched them off to the laundry for a good six hours boil. 'They'd just about stand up and walk themselves!' she declared to a pot plant on her way down. All I want to know is what am I going to wear to school tomorrow? A raincoat? A sheet? A rose between my teeth?

I could cope with all that but then when Dad comes home Ed has her angel halo on as she slaves over both the stove and the laundry at the same time and when I went in to help she said under her breath (so Dad can't hear), 'OUT!' Dad says she loses her temper like this when a patient dies. Well, all I can say is that they must be dropping like flies in that old nursing home. Probably to get some peace from her, they all lie there and pray for death so they can get some rest.

I only have to last one more day. Mum will be home. I'll be so glad to see her.

(Extract from *Black Belt* by Nicole Plüss, Angus & Robertson, Sydney)

LANGUAGE FEATURES

writer is a emotionally involved, and so language is direct and personal

language is informal (not the cool, calm and careful writing of assignment writing)

it is written in the first person ('I', 'me', 'my' etc.)

dramatic verbs

exaggeration

rhetorical questions *(no answer required)*

colourful ***similes*** *(comparisons)*

Comprehension

1 Is Ed taking James's mother's or father's place in the household? ______________________

2 Underline the correct answer. James is staying in his room because:

a he is miserable **b** he is avoiding Ed **c** he is writing his diary

3 Underline which of the following best describes Ed's visit to James's room.

a casual **b** provocative **c** friendly **d** unfriendly

4 Who is Vicious? ______________________

5 How is Ed's relationship with James (the diarist) different from Ed's relationship with his father?

____

____

6 What is Ed's usual occupation? ______________________

7 What is the immediate problem James has with Ed? ______________________

____

8 Is this problem the real one James has with Ed being in his family? Explain why you think so. __________

____

Writing skills

1 Why does this piece of writing start with a date? ______________________

2 Underline the correct answer. The first line of this diary entry contains:

a a rhetorical exclamation **b** an address **c** a piece of dialogue

3 Paragraph 2 begins in the present and switches to the past. Why?______________________

____

4 Underline the correct answer. In paragraph 4 *marched them off* suggests Ed's mood is:

a definite **b** determined **c** hesitant **d** uncompromising

5 Why has the writer used the image of *little blasts of steam* to suggest Ed's rising anger? __________

____

6 *What am I going to wear to school tomorrow?* is an example of …

a a simple question **b** a rhetorical question

7 What two words tell us Ed changes her behaviour in front of James's father? ______________________

8 Which sentence lets us know Ed loses her temper often? ______________________

9 Choose the correct answer. James refers to himself as 'I', so we can say a diary is written in the:

a first person **b** second person **c** third person

10 Which paragraph could be described as the most personal in this entry? Why? ______________________

____

11 Which words describe James's tone of voice in this diary entry?

a calm **b** exaggerated **c** measured **d** outrageous
e balanced **f** emotional **g** humorous **h** sarcastic

12 Which words describe the change of tone in the last paragraph?

a sad **b** angry **c** resigned
d quiet **e** hopeful

Vocabulary

complete	hoping	argue	hygienic	coming
drawer	laundry	patient	probably	pray

Using the Look, Cover, Write, Check method, learn these words. Underline and pay special attention to the spelling of *hygienic* and *patient*.

Focus on punctuation

Full stops and abbreviations

A full stop marks the point of abbreviation in a word, unless the shortened word is a person's name, e.g. *Maj. John Sweeney retired from the Army on 31 May; Jo (Joanne) Mills*

Full stops also follow initials but are generally omitted these days, e.g. *Mark J. Davidson/Mark J Davidson, K.P. Smith/KP Smith*

Acronyms and commonly used abbreviations do not use full stops, e.g. ADF *(Australian Defence Force),* DFAT *(Department of Foreign Affairs and Trade), CEO* (*Chief Executive Officer*)

Add full stops where necessary:

1 H J Adams Pty Ltd has expanded its premises

2 Rev John Flynn established the Flying Doctor Service

3 Capt James Cook was master of the *Endeavour.*

4 Ed was just in one of those moods

5 She gained her B Sc from Sydney University

6 I wrote to Mr and Mrs Georgiou last night

7 Benbow and Assocs have just merged with Brierley and Co to their mutual advantage

8 Gov Gen Sir Ninian Stephen later assisted with peace talks in Northern Ireland

Select a word

Choose **synonyms** (words that mean the same) from the vocabulary list.

1 whole ______________________

2 sick person receiving care ______________________

3 dispute ______________________

4 wishing ______________________

5 possibly ______________________

6 washing ______________________

Grammar

Compound sentences

A **compound sentence** contains two equally important ideas and two complete verbs. The two ideas are linked by joining words called **coordinating conjunctions**. *And* and *but* are the most common coordinating conjunctions. Others include *so* and *then*.

Ruth is in Year 7 and Miriam is in Year 9.
Idea 1 Coordinate Conj. Idea 2

Asiza likes swimming but Connie prefers athletics.
Idea 1 Coordinate Conj. Idea 2

1 Join these simple sentences to make a compound sentence using a coordinate conjunction.

a A cartoonist does not only illustrate. He writes text too.

____

b Leunig works in Melbourne. Wilcox works in Sydney.

____

c Franz is a German migrant. His wife Heidi comes from Austria.

____

d Franz goes out to work. Heidi works at home.

____

e Heidi may be a stay-at-home wife. Heidi is not a shy person.

____

2 Circle the correct coordinating conjunction in these sentences.

a Jai ran fast as he could and/so he could make a place in the finals.

b He was caught in the rain but/so he came home soaked and cold.

c Mrs Watson put a cake in the oven then/and/so went out and forgot about it.

d Writing needs to be legible and/so other people can read it.

e It's dark and/then it's scary so/but if we are together we will be safe.

f Unless the boys are late we will catch the train and/so/then/but can we rely on them?

Word study

1 From the vocabulary list write a word that means clean and germ-free. ________________

2 Look at its spelling. What two letters follow 'g'? ____________

3 This spelling pattern is common. Write these 'ie' words:

a to trust what you hear: bel_ _ve **b** to regain or recover: retr _ _ve **c** to reach a goal: ach _ _ve

4 The exception to this spelling pattern occurs after the letter 'c'. The spelling pattern 'ei' follows 'c'. Write these 'ei' words:

a a slip of paper proving that you have paid for what you bought: rec _ _ pt

b to trick: dec _ _ve

c a person who sorts out the affairs of a bankrupt business: rec _ _ver

d to bring into being: conc _ _ ve

5 Circle the words spelt incorrectly.

a conciet **b** siege **c** reciept

d deciet **e** sieve

Word usage

1 Read the following diary entry. Fill the blanks with appropriate words from the list.

shouldn't, out, have, through, to know, value, teasing, any more

FRIDAY 13

Knew I ______________ have got up this morning. Keithy annoyed me all ______________ breakfast with his ______________ about my missing out on my silver licence yesterday. How was I ______________ that stationary bus was going to pull ______________ in front of me?

Period 3 Old Bones said I'd ______________ to buy a new calculator because half of my functions don't work ______________. At $15 I reckon that's too dear. A Justin Bieber CD is better ______________ for my money than a calculator.

Note: The words underlined in the diary entry are commonly confused with their homonyms (words that sound the same but are spelt differently). Common confusions are:

- *stationery* (paper goods) and *stationary* (not moving) *Think e/envelope, a/at a stop
- *licence* (an official permit) and *license* (to permit) * Think c/card, s/sign a paper
- *annoy* (irritate) and *aggravate* (to make worse)
- *dear* (beloved or expensive) and *deer* (a species of grazing animal).

Other words that may confuse are:

- *bought* (from *buy*) and *brought* (from *bring*)
- *practice* (an activity) and *practise* (to do something several times to master it)
- *hanged* and *hung* (both are the past tense of the verb *hang*, but pictures are hung and only people are hanged).

2 Circle the correct word.

a The Under-12s are practising/practicing the art of the dribble in football.

b Mr Smith and Mr Ibrahim bought/brought ice creams for the cyclists.

c Young Pete's violin practise/practice is hard on the ears of listeners.

d Farmers are happy when they have safely bought/brought in the harvest.

3 Circle the correct word.

a He bought a new supply of exam stationary/stationery from the newsagency.

b Peter has just earned his provisional driver's licence/license.

c Don't scratch a mozzie bite. It will only aggravate/annoy the rash.

d My father thinks the concert prices are too deer/dear.

e The green car was stationery/stationary at the time of the accident.

4 Write an appropriate word in the space.

a The ______________ of waxing surfboards grew out of the need for a smooth ride.

b A veterinary __________________ is often as busy as a doctor's.

c Have you ________________ your hat with you? It's going to be very hot.

d If you ______________ cutting corners on your bike you will eventually fall off.

e Charlie ___________ a picture of the Battle of Trafalgar on his wall.

f Ned Kelly was ____________ in Melbourne Gaol.

Quick think

All words say something but some say it better than others—more precisely, more clearly.

a troop	**b** gaggle	**c** pod	**d** pack	**e** school
f flight	**g** mob	**h** shoal	**i** litter	**j** pride

Select the correct words from the list above.

1 a bunch of puppies ____________________

2 a lot of whales ____________________

3 a gang of lions ____________________

4 a herd of kangaroos ____________________

5 a group of wolves ____________________

6 a heap of monkeys ____________________

7 a stack of flying ducks ____________________

8 heaps and heaps of tiny fish ____________________

9 a gathering of sharks ____________________

10 a flock of geese ____________________

Proofreading

Correct the misspellings in this diary entry.

Yesterday I dived into the creek to retreive a ball I'd lost. Mum could not beleive I had been so silly. I know the creek is not hygenic but I was in and out in a flash so I thought I'd be all right. 'Don't be decieved,' Mum roused. 'Bacteria can get into a nick or graze faster than you would beleeve.' She was releived of her anxiety when I went and scrubbed up to be sure I was not in reciept of a batch of Slack Creek germs.

____

____

____

Idiom

Explain:

1 Susan will be <u>in hot water</u> at home tonight. ______________________________

____

2 He looks like <u>the cat that got the cream</u>. ______________________________

____

Writing paragraphs and whole texts

1 Write a brief diary entry with today's date describing an incident that has left you feeling unfairly treated. The words in the box may help you with ideas and expression.

frustrated	teased	blamed	punish	detention
fault	injustice	lonely	grim	betrayed

2 Sometimes diary entries are thoughtful or fanciful, and stem from something that you have noticed, e.g. tracks in the sand on an empty beach, the vapour trail left by a plane or the strange green light that precedes a storm.

Write a diary entry related to the sight of a cobweb clinging to your CD player. You might include the spider, how long the web has been there, how well or how poorly it has been spun, whether you like it or are disturbed or even ashamed by its presence, whether you have listened to a CD for a while, whether you have tidied your room lately etc.

3 Write a thoughtful diary entry relating to one of the following.

a a photograph of your best friend

b a private ambition

c a secret fear

d thoughts prompted by a song you have just been listening to

You could begin with words like these:

- *I wonder …*
- *I'd really hate anyone to know that …*
- *That's not the best photograph ever taken but …*

4 Write a complaining entry about something you really hate, e.g.

a something you have been told since you were in kindergarten
b the annoying habit of someone close to you
c a chore you think someone else should do
d an item of clothing you have to wear

____

____

____

____

____

____

____

5 Write about something for which you would really like an explanation, beginning with the line:
I wish someone could explain to

____

____

____

____

____

6 Put yourself in the place of a mouse who lives in the same house as a cat. Write the mouse's diary account of one day in his life in this house.

____

____

____

____

____

____

____

____

Chapter test

1 Circle the correct coordinating conjunction to link these two sentences.

then   and   so   but

a The kangaroo joey was tired.   **b** He climbed back into his mother's pouch.

2 Which sentence is correctly punctuated? __

a Pres Joan Banks addressed the board of Hold and Todd Pty Ltd
b Pres. Joan Banks addressed the board of Hold and Todd Pty Ltd.
c Pres. Joan Banks addressed the board of Hold and Todd Pty. Ltd.
d Pres Joan Banks addressed the board of Hold and Todd Pty. Ltd.

CHAPTER 3

Personal letter

STRUCTURE

address of writer and date of writing

greeting/salutation

introduction:
- *reason for letter being written*
- *includes lead-in sentence (short) laying basis for rest of paragraph*

body of letter
- *several ideas in this letter*
- *one paragraph per idea*

conclusion:
- *returns to reason for writing the letter*
- *includes some personal connection with reader*

expression of farewell and signature of writer

4/67 Fifield Lane
Ultimo 2007
22.6.13

Dear Sami,

Just a quick note to tell you we'll be away in the last week of July. My cousin's having his twenty-first birthday in Newcastle and we're all going. We'll be there for the best part of that week.

I know we were going to see the Johnny Depp film that week if it's still running but this is a family 'do' and so I really have to go. Perhaps we could go on Saturday week and make a whole day of it, that is, of course, provided you're not working.

My job's not much fun, shelf-stacking and message running, but it pays better than I'd hoped; so I can't complain. I work alternate nights, 6–10 pm.

Have your hours been shortened yet? Twenty hours a week in your HSC year is a bit rough especially when it's a job that has you on the go all the time like yours in that fast-food place.

Give me a ring if you have a better idea about the Johnny Depp film. I really do want to see that film and not just because it will be the fifth Johnny Depp film I've seen. Don't laugh! I'm not the one who sits up till 2 am watching reruns of 'Seinfeld'.

Cheers
Ruth

LANGUAGE FEATURES

tone of letter—warm, friendly; allows friendship to show through

reader is writer's close friend, and so writing is informal and conversational

abbreviated words

direct questions

***colloquial** (everyday) expressions*

direct order: evidence of friendship

Comprehension

1 Underline the correct answer. 4/67 tells us Ruth lives in a:

a house **b** home unit **c** boarding house **d** shop residence

2 Is Ruth giving Sami reasonable notice of their change of plan? Give a reason for your answer.

____

3 Underline the correct answer. Ruth and Sami are:

a university students **b** full-time shop assistants **c** secondary students

4 What evidence do we have that Ruth has a strong sense of family obligation?

____

5 How well do Ruth and Sami know each other? Explain. ______________________________

____

6 Underline the correct answer. Shelf-stacking is:

a stacking disassembled shelving **b** placing goods on shelves for sale

c piling goods on shelves out of the way

7 Explain what Ruth means by the words: *Give me a ring.* ______________________________

8 If Ruth works *alternate nights*, does that mean she works:

a on moonlight nights **b** every second night **c** odd-numbered nights?

9 To what does the number four in the street number 4/67 refer?

Writing skills

1 What does the use of the abbreviation Sami instead of Samira indicate?

a lack of courtesy **b** carelessness **c** friendship **d** dislike

2 If you were writing to Samira's grandmother, Meriam Ibrahim, whom you have never met and who is still practising medicine, how would you begin the letter? ______________________________

3 Underline the correct answer. The phrase *the best part of that week* suggests:

a about three days **b** all week **c** Saturday and Sunday **d** four or five days

4 Why is the word '*do*' placed in inverted commas in the letter?

____

5 Choose two correct answers. The style of language used in this letter is:

a formal (very proper) **b** colloquial (conversational) **c** incisive (cutting) **d** informal

6 Find two examples of colloquial expression in paragraph 4.

a ______________________________ **b** ______________________________

7 Underline the correct answer. The sentence *Don't laugh!* suggests past conversations between the girls might have been about:

a Johnny Depp **b** Seinfeld

8 Circle the correct answer. The effect of this sentence is to emphasise:

a their close friendship **b** the fact that they often go to the pictures **c** they rarely see each other

9 Choose which of the following endings would be unsuitable for use in this letter.

a See you **b** Bye for now **c** Your friend **d** Yours faithfully

Vocabulary

recipient	**address**	**margin**	**greeting**	**salutation**
information	**inquiry**	**invitation**	**complaint**	**signature**

Remember the Look, Cover, Write, Check method. Notice that 'q' is always followed by 'u'. Underline this and highlight the 'g' in signature to help you remember them.

The ending *~tion* (*invitation, salutation*) is very common. Mastery of this ending will make learning big words easy.

Focus on punctuation

Capitals and full stops

Insert capitals and full stops in the following.

australians come from many different races and cultures but they are one people australians celebrate this fact on australia day on january 26 in a uniquely australian way local communities gather together around a barbecue to celebrate being australian and to honour those people who have helped improve the lives of their fellow citizens

Select a word

Choose words from the vocabulary list that mean the same as these words.

1 origin of letter ____________________ **2** data ____________________

3 query ____________________ **4** greeting ____________________

5 location ________________ **6** border ________________

Grammar

Subordinate conjunctions

Remember: Coordinate conjunctions *and, but, so* and *then* join two complete ideas of equal importance in a compound sentence.

Subordinate conjunctions also join two complete ideas into one sentence, a **complex sentence**. In this kind of sentence one idea is always more important than the other. Subordinate conjunctions include *when, while, although, because* and *unless*, e.g.

We eat the fish we catch <u>when</u> we go camping.
Subordinate conjunction

<u>While</u> we were still unpacking the rain poured down.
Subordinate conjunction

Subordinate conjunctions not only occur in the middle of a sentence; they can also start a sentence,
e.g. *<u>Unless</u> the weather is bad we will go fishing tomorrow.*

1 Circle the subordinate conjunctions.

a I didn't want to go unless Angela came too.
b When Mr Bush was promoted his whole family celebrated.
c The animals were restless although they had already been fed.
d He was tired because he had run the cross country race.
e Margie stroked the python although she was scared of reptiles.

2 Underline the coordinate conjunctions.

a I was reluctant to go and had to be persuaded to set out.
b The wind howled, the rain poured down and the thunder rolled but the band played on.
c Lightning flashed, then thunder crashed in the heavens.
d Lal slowed his pace so his little brother could catch up.

3 Join the following simple sentences with coordinate conjunctions to make compound sentences.

a He won. He did not win fairly.

____

b Enzo can swing on a trapeze. He can also walk a tightrope.

____

c Rain is pouring down. The washing will not dry.

____

d The sheep ate the grass. The sheep ate all the flowers in the garden.

____

4 Join the following with subordinate conjunctions to make complex sentences.

a The train is late. We will catch a bus.

____

b The ferry drifted from the wharf. A passenger fell into the harbour.

____

c We would like to go for a walk. It is raining.

____

d You are bitten by a snake. Bandage the site firmly and see a doctor.

____

Word study

1 Complete the following using words from the vocabulary list.

a A letter should always have an ______________ on the right-hand side of the page.

b The ______________ of a letter of invitation is usually delighted.

c It is wise to keep a copy of a letter of ______________ about a shoddy product.

d *Dear Elizabeth* would not be an appropriate ______________ on a letter to the Queen of England.

e Enclosed you will find the ______________ you requested about the Internet.

2 The suffix *~ee* often indicates the person who is the object of some action, e.g.

One who is interviewed = interviewee

Complete the following using this pattern.

a One to whom a letter is addressed is an ______________ .

b One to whom a house is leased is a ______________ .

c One who has had a leg amputated is an ______________ .

3 Complete these *~tion* words.

a extreme happiness e x _ l _ _ tion

b blood movement c _ _ c _ _ _ tion

c buses, trains, etc. t _ _ _ sp _ _ _ _ tion

d keeping safe c _ _ s _ _ v _ tion

e wildlife park r _ s _ _ v _ tion

f a complete turn r _ t _ tion

g leisure activity r _ c _ _ _ tion

h a new thing i _ _ _ v _ tion

Word usage

1 Correctly set out this address.

a 33 Great North Road Abbotsford NSW 2046 **a** ______________________

____

____

____

b Write the correct form of greeting to your cousin, Jason. **b** ______________________

____

c Write the correct form of greeting to your school Principal, Charles Bowden. **c** ______________________

2 These are appropriate letter endings. Write T (True) or F (False).

a to your family doctor: Cheers, __________

b to your best friend: May the force be with you, __________

c to your father: Yours sincerely, __________

d to your employer: Yours faithfully, __________

e to your clergyman: Yours sincerely, __________

3 Match the colloquial expressions on the left with the explanations on the right.

a	a daredevil	**i**	a message sent by mobile phone
b	a backpacker	**ii**	a self-taken photograph
c	a text	**iii**	someone who takes risks
d	a selfie	**iv**	a tourist who travels lightly

4 Write F (Formal) or C (Colloquial) beside each one.

a Rack off, mate. I'm busy. __________

b Would you mind shifting your bag, please. __________

c By the sound of it they're having a ball! __________

d Their pleasure was evident in the smiles they exchanged. __________

Quick think

1 A person who is skilled/learned in a particular area is a *~ist*, e.g. *specialist*. Complete the names of the specialists to match their subject areas.

	Subject area	*Specialists*
a	eyes	op _ _ _ _ _ _ _ _ _ _ ist
b	earth tremors	se _ _ _ _ _ _ _ ist
c	life forms	bio _ _ _ ist
d	volcanoes	vul _ _ _ _ _ _ _ ist
e	rocks	ge _ _ _ _ ist

2 Other *~ist* people:

a one who dislikes other people: misan _ _ _ _ _ _ _ _

b one who terrorises with violence: ter _ _ _ _ _ _

c one who is your opponent: antag _ _ _ _ _

d one who dislikes women: mis _ _ _ _ _ _ _

Proofreading

Correct all misspelt words.

information, recipiant, inqiry, margin, saluatation, sinature, adress, invitation.

____

____

Idiom

Explain:

1 That child is full of beans today. ______________________

____

2 Aargh, don't give me that. You knew what you had to do. ______________________

____

Writing paragraphs and whole texts

1 You wish to convey the following information in a letter to a friend you are inviting to a concert. Number each item 1, 2 or 3 according to which paragraph you would put it in your three-paragraph letter.

a ___ venue

b ___ date and time of concert

c ___ name of concert

d ___ transport arrangements

e ___ invitation

f ___ meeting place

g ___ meeting time

h ___ suggestion for a meal before the concert

2 Insert the following correctly on this letter.

a your address

b Yours sincerely

c Dear Mr Rugova

d date

e an X where the first sentence of the letter will begin

f all necessary punctuation

3 Write a two-paragraph letter to your school Principal. Ask if your year may go on an excursion to the Snowy Mountains. Suggest that you could travel by bus and that accommodation is available at a reasonable price in Jindabyne. Tell him/her that Mr Hunt and Mrs Jovanovic are happy to supervise, as are some parents. Explain that this excursion will be a field study as required by your geography course. Assure him/her that all students will conduct themselves properly on the excursion.

Make sure your letter is set out correctly and write formally, not colloquially.

4 Write a letter of thanks to your grandparents for a birthday gift OR a letter to a friend suggesting a camping trip. Be specific, so the recipient knows exactly what you are talking about, and don't forget appropriate salutations and signatures.

Chapter test

1 Circle the correct subordinate conjunction to link these two sentences.

if when although because

a I cannot get into the house. **b** I left the key inside.

2 Mark ✗ where you would put a full stop to make two complete sentences.

Clinton hit the ball for six but no one saw it they were all watching the snake on the pitch.

CHAPTER 4

Factual recount

STRUCTURE

introduction: *contains the key elements of the story—dogs and rabbits*

body of story:
- *recounts what happened in sequence*
- *each development in the story in a new paragraph*

conclusion:
- *sums up the happiness*
- *'good news' account of the rabbit rescue*

Ellie adopts bunny brood

LONDON: When most dogs see a rabbit their reaction is to chase it down the nearest hole.

But in the case of Ellie, the cavalier king charles spaniel, it brought out her motherly instinct.

Ellie has 'adopted' four orphaned rabbits found starving next to their burrow by her owner, Sara Reynolds.

The dog is fiercely protective, cleaning and playing with them. When they are tired, they crawl under her fur to sleep.

Ms Reynolds, 28, found the orphans, whose mother was probably taken by a fox, at the end of her garden in Lodsworth, Sussex.

'They were so skinny,' she said. 'It was very sad, so I brought them inside.

'The next day Ellie decided they were hers.

'She hopped up onto the table when I was feeding them and curled up beside them. She really is their surrogate mother now.

'She won't let anyone near them, especially men.'

Because the rabbits are fed on goat's milk every two hours Ms Reynolds has to take them to school, where she is a singing teacher, and Ellie insists on going too.

The dog and rabbits are left in an empty classroom, then at break-times Ms Reynolds feeds them.

'The arrival of the animals at school has caused quite a commotion,' she said.

'There is a lot of singing going on at the moment.'

Sunday Telegraph

LANGUAGE FEATURES

tells what happened; does not try to re-create the incident; the reader must know what happened but does not need to share the experience

written in third person ('he', 'she', 'it' etc.)

several facts included in each sentence

factual writing—little emotion involved
- *all statements; no questions*
- *all short sentences*
- *minimum adjectives—verbs do the work, e.g. 'insists'*

Comprehension

1 Circle where this report comes from.

a Scotland **b** England **c** Wales **d** Ireland

2 Who rescued the orphaned rabbits from starvation? ______________________________

3 Underline the correct answer. A burrow is:

a a nest in a thorny bush **b** a hollow in a tree trunk **c** an underground tunnel

4 Underline the correct answer. The rabbits were rescued out of a sense of:

a pity **b** duty **c** tidiness **d** vermin control

5 List two reasons for describing Ellie as the rabbits' surrogate mother. ______________________

____

6 Why does Sara Reynolds take the rabbits to school? ______________________

7 *Ellie insists on going too.* How do you think Ellie *insists*? ______________________

8 Circle the most precise answer. Ellie's care for the animals is so unusual because:

a they are not her own young
b they are undernourished
c they are of a different species
d Ms Reynolds is caring for them very well

9 Ms Reynolds's words *There is a lot of singing going on at the moment* suggest:

a the rabbits are singing
b Ellie, the rabbits and Ms Reynolds are singing
c the whole school is happy

Writing skills

1 Write down two things about the layout of the extract that prove it is a newspaper report.

____

2 Is the connection between paragraphs 1 and 2 contrast or comparison? ______________________

3 Why is the word '*adopted*' in inverted commas? ______________________

____

4 Like many headlines (newspaper story titles) this one is **ambiguous**; i.e. it has more than one possible meaning. What are its two meanings? ______________________

____

5 The word *insists* covers a lot of meaning. This is an example of what type of writing?

a lazy **b** compact **c** vague **d** complex

6 The term *surrogate* tells us that Ms Reynolds is ______________________

7 Underline the correct answer. This report is intended to:

a inform **b** entertain **c** question **d** challenge

8 To retell this story, what fact would be most important to include in your recounting?

____

9 Underline the correct answer. The fact in question 8 is most important because it is:

a an interesting fact **b** the main point of the story
c an unusual fact **d** an absurd point in the story

10 How would you describe this news story?

a a serious report **b** trivia **c** a good news story

Vocabulary

sympathy	excitement	anxiety	empathy	anticipation
pity	sorrow	concentration	envy	jealousy

1. Practise spelling words that contain vowel combinations, e.g. *jealousy*.
2. Break up long words into syllables to help you learn them, e.g. *con-cen-tra-tion*. Spell these syllables out aloud to impress them on your memory.

Focus on punctuation

Correct these sentences using capitals, full stops and question and exclamation marks.

1. John cried out 'where's my skateboard'
2. The kelly gang robbed the braidwood bank and escaped shouting 'you won't catch us'
3. 'Boom' sounded the great cannon at midday
4. capt henry matson asked if the third watch had been relieved
5. Harvey hissed, 'don't move there's a snake next to your foot'
6. 'watch out' the rigger shouted as the beam crashed to the footpath
7. 'man overboard' the cry ran the length of the ship
8. why are all the clocks stopped at 10.45
9. his royal highness, prince fergus george, shouted 'Off with his head'

Select a word

Find synonyms in the vocabulary list for the following.

1. grief ____________________
2. concern ____________________
3. compassion ____________________
4. enthusiasm ____________________
5. attention ____________________
6. forward thinking ____________________

Grammar

Questions (?) and exclamations (!)

A **question** is a sentence that asks for an answer, e.g.
Will you contribute to the Freedom from Hunger appeal?

An **exclamation** is a dramatic or heavily emphasised sentence, e.g.
'Rats are vermin!' declared the Health Inspector.

Sometimes a question is not asked directly. Such an indirect question is followed by a full stop, e.g.
Direct question: *Will Mr Giles be the new cricket coach?*
Indirect question: *He wanted to know if Mr Giles would be the new cricket coach.*

1 Punctuate the following with ? or !

e.g. *Where is the Adele CD?*
Adele's a fabulous singer!

- **a** 'Thief ____ ' shouted the old lady.
- **b** 'Stand at ease ____ ' bellowed the sergeant major.
- **c** 'Which way did he go ____ ' called the policeman.
- **d** 'Please sir, may I have some more ____ ' asked Oliver Twist.
- **e** 'That's absolutely ridiculous ____ ' declared the instructor.

2 Write E (Exclamation) or Q (Question) after each of the following.

- **a** He listened carefully and then asked, 'But what is it for?' ____
- **b** When the concert was over they wandered home exclaiming, 'That was fantastic!' ____
- **c** After I accidentally smashed an ornament the shopkeeper shouted, 'You'll have to pay for that!' ____
- **d** 'That dolphin will die! You have to untangle it from the net!' the woman screamed. ____

3 Add the end punctuation and write D (Direct) or I (Indirect) after each sentence.

- **a** He had no reply to his inquiry about the arrival time of the plane from Fiji ____
- **b** Did you forget your sports gear again ____
- **c** Jemal wanted to know how many planets there are in the solar system ____
- **d** I am inquiring about the whereabouts of a missing sports car ____

Word study

1 The words in the vocabulary list all refer to particular emotions. Match vocabulary list words to these emotional states.

- **a** identifying with someone else's situation ____________
- **b** being unusually happy and active ____________
- **c** feeling a deep sadness ____________
- **d** sharing the hurt of another person ____________
- **e** being mentally fixed on an activity ____________
- **f** feeling sorry for someone ____________
- **g** wanting what belongs to another ____________
- **h** being worried ____________
- **i** looking forward to something ____________

2 Complete these sentences using words from the vocabulary list.

- **a** Ellie devoted her total ____________ to the rabbits.
- **b** The tiny rabbits' ____________ about their future must have been great.
- **c** Sara Reynolds's ____________ for the orphan rabbits led her to save them.
- **d** An atmosphere of ____________ prevailed in the school when the orphan rabbits arrived.

3 Choose a word from the list to describe the state of mind in each situation, e.g.
Peter is studying. He doesn't hear someone come into the room. Concentration

- **a** Penny winced when she heard the dentist's drill bite into her tooth. ____________
- **b** Tears came to William's eyes when he heard the orphan lamb bleat for its mother. ____________
- **c** Ten, nine eight ... Marcus fidgeted excitedly as he waited for the blastoff. ____________
- **d** People lined the bank as the river level rose even closer to the last flood level. ____________

Evaluating other people's writing

Dog mothers rabbits

A small English dog called Ellie has taken over the care of four baby rabbits. The rabbits were found starving outside their burrow by a schoolteacher who felt sorry for them and took them home.

As she cared for them, Ellie became interested and now protects them. She curls up with them to warm them, cleans them when necessary and plays with them.

Above is a recount of the report at the beginning of this chapter. Read it and then write down two other essential facts that have been left out.

1 ______________________________

2 ______________________________

Word usage

1 Match these words to their meanings and fill in the blanks: pups, joeys, cubs, calves, goslings, kits

- **a** Baby rabbits are ____________
- **b** Baby whales are ____________
- **c** Baby kangaroos are ____________
- **d** Baby bears are ____________
- **e** Baby geese are ____________
- **f** Baby seals are ____________

2 Choose the appropriate alternative.

- **a** Lionesses hunt/rear their cubs alone. ____________
- **b** It is uncommon for one species to act as lawful/surrogate parents for another. ____________
- **c** Meerkat young are raised in the community/society by all members of the clan. ________
- **d** Solitary/lonely animals are more independent than flock or herd animals. ________
- **e** Flock/herd/mob birds fly in formation and turn in unison. ________

3 Insert the appropriate word from the vocabulary list.

- **a** Animals feel the same ____________ at the death of one of their young as humans do.
- **b** Animals do not ____________ others for their possessions as we do.
- **c** ____________ in their owner's absence will lead many dogs to bark incessantly.
- **d** The leopard's eyes were fixed in ____________ on the monkeys at play.
- **e** Young wolves are ____________ of the pack leader's favouring one over another.

Quick think

1 Complete these proverbs.

- **a** Neither a borrower nor a ____________ be.
- **b** Spare the rod and spoil the ____________ .
- **c** The proof of the ____________ is in the eating.
- **d** A stitch in time saves ____________ .
- **e** Too many ________ spoil the broth.
- **f** Pride goes before a ____________.

2 Match the proverbs in Exercise 1 to their messages below.

- **a** For a good job you need only a few workers. _____
- **b** Discipline children. _____

c You are no more important than you seem to be. ______

d Believe only what you can test to be true. ______

e Do tasks promptly. ______

f Be responsible and prudent. ______

Proofreading

Correct spelling and punctuation. Make your corrections on the passage itself.

> In old australia orphan lambs were razed in a wooden box with a whole in the side. Outside the box a you who's own lamb had died was short-tethered to a post close to the box hole. She coold here the lamb's sad cry, 'baa baa', but not see it. The lamb cood put its head threw the whole, find the sheep's udder and drink. even tho sheep do not except lambs that are not their own in this way an orphan lamb could be savd.

Idiom

Explain:

1 John: I'm coming.
James: Yeah, so is Christmas! ______________________________

____

2 Shake a leg, Fred. We'll be late. ______________________________

____

Writing paragraphs and whole texts

1 Read the following and in your own words recount (retell) what you read. Include only essential facts and write in full sentences.

> A break and enter occurred in Orion Street about midnight on 30 May. The resident awoke to a noise at a front window and heard footsteps in the house; her two small children were asleep at the time. Since she did not get up to investigate until morning, it was 7 am when she found the front window had been forced open and items displaced although nothing was stolen.

____

____

____

____

____

____

____

2

Too much honey for popstar

The hectic life of a British popstar has taken its toll on 16-year-old Billie Piper, who has cancelled the remainder of her Australian tour.

The teenage pop princess, who has been promoting her hit single 'Honey to the Bee', was yesterday holed up in her city hotel with a virus.

A spokeswoman said Billie was 'absolutely devastated' but the busy schedule had left their star talent almost without a voice.

'She stayed in bed on Sunday and is really upset that she won't be able to meet all of her fans,' she told *Thirteen* yesterday.

Billie was to have given a showcase performance at the Grand Hyatt last night and to have made an appearance in Mount Druitt today.

List the facts in this story as if you were making notes for a recounting (retelling) of it. Write in point form, not complete sentences, e.g. *Piper's Australian tour cancelled mid-season.*

a ______________________________

b ______________________________

c ______________________________

d ______________________________

e ______________________________

f ______________________________

g ______________________________

h ______________________________

3 Choose one of the following incidents:

i a car smash at traffic lights

ii the rescue of a child who fell in the water between a ferry and the wharf

iii a bank robbery

iv the rescue of a cat from the top of a telegraph pole

Write down a list of six things about this incident in the order they occurred.

____

____

____

____

____

____

4 A fire occurred at your school during period 4. This necessitated a complete evacuation of the premises. Write the story of the fire and the evacuation as a factual recount. Include site and progress of the fire, first discovery of the fire, alarm and evacuation procedures, emergency personnel attending, any health problems associated with the fire, damage caused and a comment from the school Principal about the situation.

____

____

____

____

____

____

____

____

____

____

____

____

____

____

____

____

____

____

____

____

____

Chapter test

1 Circle the correctly spelt word.

a anxitey **b** anticpation **c** consentration **d** excitement

2 Which sentence is correctly punctuated? __

a Why is your hair green today.

b Why is your hair Green today?

c Why is your hair green today!

d Why is your hair green today?

CHAPTER 5

Narrative

STRUCTURE

introduction:
- *includes lead-in (**topic**) sentence*
- *supplies background to body of narrative to suggest it is strange*

body of story: *tells the story with each part of the story in a separate paragraph; paragraphs arranged chronologically (in order of happening)*

conclusion: *tells the consequences of what happened in the body of the story*

No one knew how deep the water was. Some said it went all the way to the centre of the earth. Felix had walked here on Saturday with his brother and sister, and Ramon had said without thinking, 'I'd never go in there', and this had made Felix wonder if he was brave enough to dive into the quarry's flooded depths.

As the breeze ruffled the surface into wavelets, Felix inched his toes forward. He was twelve years old, and looked small and frail at the cliff edge. The breeze stroked his hair. His school uniform was in a heap beside his bag; he was wearing blue swimming shorts.

He closed his eyes, inhaled deeply and jumped.

His entry sent up a high splash, and waves hurried to hit the walls of the quarry.

One minute passed … then another, and another … Thirty minutes … forty-five. Longer than any boy can hold his breath.

Then a hand shot up, fingers rigid, followed by an arm and a head. Not gasping for air, not even the slightest bit out of breath, Felix swam with calm strokes, and climbed from the quarry without once looking back.

(Extract from Chapter 1 of *Moxiana* by Michael Stephens, HarperCollins, Sydney)

LANGUAGE FEATURES

narrative does more than recounting; it creates an experience the reader shares with its characters; therefore it contains description and atmosphere as well as fact

background details about what has been said and thought about the quarry

word picture of Felix so we can see him

dramatic description of action; note effective verbs in simple past tense suspense/tension shown in timing and punctuation

conclusion shows quarry has changed Felix; compare introduction and conclusion: Felix wondered in introduction but swims with calm strokes and does not look back in conclusion

Comprehension

1 Underline the correct answer. A quarry is a:

a sinkhole **b** prey **c** blowhole **d** stone-mining excavation

2 This happened on a weekday. Is this statement true or false? ______________________

3 The first paragraph suggests that Felix feels insecure about something. What is it?

____

____

4 What evidence do we have that the water was a long way below the cliff top?

______

5 What is strange about what we read in paragraph 5? ______

______

6 What can you conclude about Felix's underwater experience? ______

______

Writing skills

1 What phrase in paragraph 1 tells us that the bottom of the quarry is abnormally deep?

______

2 Underline the correct answer. Wavelets are:

a small waves **b** circular ripples **c** boat wash

3 **a** Fill in the missing letters. We are not told how tall Felix is, so the phrase *small and frail* is really telling us more about how tall the _ _ _ _ _ is than about how short Felix is.

b Is this an example of direct or indirect description? ______

4 In which paragraph is Felix challenged to the dive? ______

5 How does the writer show us that Felix had planned this dive? ______

______

6 Underline the correct answer. Paragraph 3 is very short. Why? The writer:

a wanted to dramatise the action **b** wanted to suggest tension

c had nothing else to say **d** both a and b

7 What word suggests the speed of Felix's surfacing? ______

8 Paragraph 1 suggests uncertainty. What sentence in the last paragraph suggests Felix has found confidence. ______

9 Underline the correct answer/s. Linking the first and last paragraphs in this way is an example of:

a good planning **b** lazy writing

c developing character depth **d** unnecessary plot and detail

10 Underline the correct answer. Using this text as an example, narrative writing is usually written:

a chronologically **b** haphazardly **c** in thought form **d** as a series of descriptions

11 Stephens does not describe Felix but by the end of this passage we know a lot about him.

List four things we know that are unrelated to the actual dive.

______ ______

______ ______

12 Consider the text carefully. Which is more important in narrative: description or events and incidents (what happens)? ______

Vocabulary

recount	relate	narrate	retell	suggest
quarry	rigid	inhale	exhale	slightest

A helpful spelling method is to group words with the same spelling pattern, e.g. *narrate* and *relate*, and learn them together.

Focus on punctuation

Commas (,)

Commas:

- separate items in a list, e.g.
  I bought pens, pencils, a compass and a protractor.
- separate a series of activities, e.g.
  In the mornings I swam, in the afternoons I fished, in the evenings I went for a walk and at night I slept like a baby.

Note: *and* replaces a comma between the last two items in a list.

1 Insert commas in the following.
e.g. *Shane, Carlos, Peter and Kenji went swimming.*

a The chips were shared among Elise Simone Raelene and Katie.

b Unless every Tom Dick and Harry comes there will be no audience.

c Pack a towel swimmers sunscreen a hat and some mosquito repellent.

d The feline species includes domestic cats lions tigers leopards cheetahs cougars jaguars civets and various smaller forest dwelling cats.

2 Insert commas in the following.
e.g. *The seagulls fought, squawked, harried beachgoers and stole the catches of fishermen.*

a 'Clean your shoes find a handkerchief put on a jumper and don't be late for school,' Mum says every morning.

b Run a length of track swim an expanse of water cycle a stretch of road—they're the three parts of a triathlon.

c The old Greek Olympic Games only featured running hurdling wrestling leaping discus and javelin throwing and long jump.

d Carving bone whittling wood polishing gems and sculpting stone are ancient skills.

3 Tick the sentence that is correctly punctuated and cross (✗) those that are not.

a The wind howled the sky grew dark sheet lightning filled the sky and I was scared. ___

b The wind howled, the sky grew dark sheet lightning filled the sky and I was scared. ___

c The wind howled, the sky grew dark, sheet lightning filled the sky and I was scared. ___

d The wind howled the sky grew dark sheet lightning filled the sky, and I was scared. ___

Select a word

A story can be made more interesting by careful choice of words.

1 *Say* is a boring word. All but four of the words below can be used instead of *say*. Circle those four.

declare, deceive, announce, tell, whisper, deny, agitate, charge, accuse, gossip, inquire, damage, chat, argue, disagree, converse, escape, interrogate, whinge, shriek, reply

2 These words all describe the colour red. Can you complete them?

a sc _ _ l _ t **b** c _ _ ms _ n **c** v _ _ m _ lion **d** b _ _ g _ _ dy

3 Can you complete these words that all mean walk?

a st _ _ _ l **b** a _ _ le **c** m _ _ nd _ r **d** w _ _ d _ r

Grammar

Verbs

Verbs are activity words. They do and are things, e.g.
Jessica, who is a successful distance runner, ran the City to Surf in 78 minutes.
(is = verb; ran = verb)

1 Underline all verbs in the following.
e.g. *Harry competed in the 50-m hurdles and came sixth.*

a Peter Tranh won the 100-m sprint. **b** A gymnast trains daily for years.

2 Underline all the verbs in the following sentences from the text.

a The breeze ruffled the surface into wavelets.

b He closed his eyes, inhaled deeply and jumped.

c He was twelve years old, and looked small and frail at the cliff edge.

3 Sometimes verbs contain more than one word, e.g.
Billy Slater has played fine rugby league for several years.
(has played = verb)

Underline the complete verb in the following.

a Felix had walked here on Saturday.

b Because he had been identified the criminal surrendered to the police.

c Even if the weather is bad we will go to the P!nk concert.

4 Underline all the verbs in the following.

a Paul will play on Saturday if he recovers from the flu.

b The Pollies, a singing quartet, will be the entertainers on Friday.

c A swarm of bees has been removed from the hive they built inside a ventilator.

d I am always glad to see you, especially if you come at the weekends.

e Were you in the garden when that storm broke?

Word study

1 From the vocabulary list choose:

a two words to tell a story ____________ ____________

b two words to do with the act of breathing ____________ ____________

c a word meaning an excavation ____________

d a word meaning the same as *merest* ____________

e a word meaning stiff or unbending ____________

2 Insert appropriate words from the vocabulary list in the following.

a The rope was frozen so that it was as ____________ as a steel rod.

b Whales ____________ through their blowhole.

c If you ______________________ cigarette smoke you will damage your lungs.

d Sydney was built from sandstone cut in a nearby ___________

e I __________ you do your homework before football training.

3 Choose the correct alternative

a After you tell your story to the head teacher you will have to retell/narrate it to the Principal. ___________

b If you inhale/exhale on a cold morning your breath will fog the air. ______________________

4 The word *quarry* has a second unrelated meaning.

a Look it up in the dictionary and write the meaning here. ______________________________

b Mark with ✗ the sentence that uses *quarry* incorrectly.

i The cheetah pursued his quarry till it collapsed with exhaustion. ____

ii Sailors tossed their dirty quarry overboard for the fish. ____

iii A marble quarry is always found in limestone country. ____

Word usage

Henry's bad morning

The noise of the alarm woke him. It was not a nice noise. He did nvot want to get up but he did anyway and went to the bathroom. He dressed, which took him a long time, and went into the kitchen. He sat down. It was the chair he usually sat on. *He ate rice bubbles. * He ate toast. * He drank milk. After that he felt too full. He felt sick. When he reached the bus stop there was no one there. He had missed the bus. While he was still standing there thinking about what to do all of a sudden he was sick all over his shoes.

1 This story contains underlined examples of poor narrative style. Complete these text improvements.

a Replace *nice* with unpl _ _ _ _ _ _, delete the negative __________ and change *a* to __________.

b Replace *went* with a more interesting and appropriate word from the following:

i walked ii wandered iii ran iv marched

c Combine the two underlined sentences into one. ______________________________

____

d Combine the three *marked sentences into one using the word *and* twice.

____

e Replace the final underlined phrase with a single word. ______________________________

f Write the word from the title that should appear at least once in the story and does not. ___________

2 Replace each clumsy group of words with a single word.

e.g. *He made a loud snuffling noise as he slept.* → *He snored as he slept.*

a The cars made a steel on steel sound as they collided. sc _ _ _ ched

b A threatening dog makes an angry noise and shows its teeth. s _ _ _ ls

c Little children talk nonstop and quickly about nothing special. ch _ _ _ er

d Sam shouted with a voice that seemed to come from his belly. b _ _ _ ow _ _

e The lost pup made a sad sort of little noise. wh _ _ p _ _ ed

Quick think

Prefixes are syllables placed at the beginning of a word to change or refine its meaning, e.g. *interior* (inside), *exterior* (outside).

Using the prefixes *re~* (again), *in~* (in/into) and *ex~* (out/of) make words that mean the same as the following.

1 apply again ____________________

2 write again ____________________

3 make a new definition ____________________

4 breathe out ____________________

5 someone who is outgoing and sociable ____________________

6 keep someone out of a group activity ____________________

7 breathe in ____________________

8 one who is very shy and not interested in socialising ____________________

9 bring someone into a group activity ____________________

Proofreading

Correct spelling and punctuation where necessary.

1 peter nye was elected school captain.

2 Maria kwok has been nominated Citizen of the Year

3 yang brothers is a carpet-laying service.

4 The Fred Hollows foundation helps restore the site of blind people in asia africa and Australia.

Idiom

Explain:

1 Lucy found herself between a rock and a hard place. ____________________

____

2 When the cat's away, the mice will play. ____________________

____

Writing paragraphs and whole texts

1 Chronology sequence (arrangement of incidents in order of happening) is important in narrative.

a Arrange these foods in sequence for an Australian meal.

i sweets **ii** soup **iii** main meal **iv** coffee ____________________

b Starting with *midnight* arrange these in chronological sequence.

i dusk	**ii** dawn	**iii** midnight	**iv** midday
v twilight	**vi** afternoon	**vii** wee small hours	**viii** evening

c Arrange in order of driving activity.

i select gear	**ii** enter vehicle	**iii** switch on ignition	**iv** depress accelerator

2 Read this list of events. Rearrange and rewrite them to create a story.

a Behind them the bushfire erupted over the ridge and poured into the gully like some blazing waterfall engulfing everything in its path.

b Our gully filled with drifting mushroom-coloured smoke.

c By 10 am the wind had picked up.

d Within an hour the first spiral of smoke was sighted.

e Day broke as hot as the day before.

f With the smoke came the first sounds of the fire.

g The wind began that all too familiar high wild singing.

h Beneath it we could just hear the faint sound as if a train were roaring in the distance.

i Flocks of small birds suddenly burst out of the smoke flying crazily in their panic.

j The sun hung like a scarlet balloon in the darkening sky.

3 Powerful verbs create good narrative, e.g.

Interstate trucks thundered through the night.

Thundered suggests speed and loud noise and power—all in one word.

Use some or all of the verbs below to write six or seven lines about a boat caught in a storm at sea.

flap, surge, tower, wallow, crash, thunder, splash, topple, rip, churn, splinter

4 Write a short narrative about a yacht caught in a storm and the rescue of its crew by helicopter.

Make sure the events are arranged chronologically and that you make it sound exciting and dangerous by using strong nouns and verbs.

Chapter test

1 Circle the verb in this sentence.

Chloe peeled her apple slowly.

2 Which sentence is correctly punctuated? _____

a I love insects: grasshoppers, crickets, locusts, ladybirds and even dainty mosquitoes.

b I love insects: grasshoppers, crickets, locusts, ladybirds, and even, dainty mosquitoes.

c I love insects: grasshoppers, crickets locusts ladybirds and even dainty mosquitoes.

d I love insects: grasshoppers, crickets, locusts, ladybirds, and, even dainty mosquitoes.

3 Mark ✗ where you would put the missing comma.

That orchard grows apples pears, apricots, peaches, plums and nectarines.

CHAPTER 6

Interview

STRUCTURE

- *a series of questions followed by answers*
- *questions designed to elicit interesting information or revealing personality traits from the interviewee*

questions to discover information about Olympic swimming prospects and attitudes

questions to move interview from information towards personal revelation

questions to encourage interviewee to reveal her personality and private history

question concluding interview

Who stands between you and a gold medal at Sydney 2000?
I think I have two rivals: Penelope Heyns, who is from South Africa, in the 100-m [breast stroke] although she won both the 100 m and 200 m at Atlanta she's more a threat to me in the 100 m; and Agnes Kovacs who is Hungarian. She's quite competitive over the 200 m. At the same time there are eight people in a race and anyone can win. So I don't like to focus my attention too much on an individual. But the two I mentioned are the standouts.

Are you good friends?
I know Penny really well. I've been competing against her since '92, I think. We get on really well when we see each other at meets. We have a good chat. Kovacs, she doesn't speak a lot of English so she's quite hard to communicate with. She's learning English at school at the moment; she's only 15. She practises her English on us at meets. The more she speaks to us the more we get to know her.

So it's friendly rivalry?
Oh yes, definitely.

What do you rate as your greatest sporting achievement?
Winning the World Championships in Rome in '94. The 100-m and 200-m breast stroke and breaking the world record in the 100 m.

How do you unwind after a big race?
Going to the beach. I find hanging around water really relaxing. Obviously it's different than being at a swimming pool competing or training. I also enjoy doing the normal things I otherwise don't have time to do like going to the movies and watching TV.

What do you reckon is the smartest thing you ever did?
Learn to swim when I was seven. I was a chronic asthmatic so I was under the direction of doctors to increase my lung capacity and improve my fitness.

Did you love the water? Were you dragged there?
I was dragged big time. I didn't enjoy swimming at all when I first started. Mum would have to drag me there kicking and screaming. It took a few weeks. I had quite a bad fear of the water.

What were you like as a child?
I don't know. You would have to ask my Mum. I think I was a happy-go-lucky kid. I didn't get into serious trouble but I was probably like most kids, a bit mischievous. I didn't worry about too many things.

What is your favourite childhood memory?
We used to go on family holidays each year, usually up north somewhere, say to Great Keppel Island or around Airlie Beach or some other resort. We used to have a good time just swimming all day or going snorkelling at the reef. That was a lot of fun.

As a child, what did you dream of becoming?
Kids change their mind each week. Even now I don't really know what sort of direction "I would like to take after my swimming is finished. I probably would have studied something. I don't know what—I like kids but I couldn't see myself as a teacher.

What do you look for in a friend?
Someone you can trust and someone you can have a pretty good laugh with. So, probably a sense of humour and someone who is caring.

What makes you angry?
Making coffee and then going to the fridge and there's no milk. Ha! I hate black coffee too, so that really makes me angry.

What are your most treasured possessions?
Photo albums. They're irreplaceable. I have a pretty big collection. A lot from swimming trips, the Olympics, family, friends.

And your biggest regret?
I don't think I have any regrets because anything I have done wrong I have always learnt a really good lesson from it. There's nothing I would change in my life because every lesson I have learnt has been really valuable.

Okay—last question—surprise us, tell us something we don't know about you?
Ummm—I can't cook.

(Extract from an interview with Olympic swimmer Samantha Riley by Anthony Raineri in *Total Sports Magazine*)

LANGUAGE FEATURES

- *because the interviewee is the subject of the interview she must have the bulk of the text*
- *therefore interviewer's questions must be short, prepared and to the point*

question seeking fact about Olympic prospects

question confirming previous answer and prodding for more information

question seeking emotional response about Olympic prospect

return to pure fact question style

colloquial (everyday) language in questions—designed to make interviewee feel at ease

questions to establish:
- *past*
- *present*
- *future*

question to provoke character revelation

Comprehension

1 Penny Heyns is a more threatening competitor to Sam Riley in the 200 m than in the 100 m. Is this true or false? ______________________________

2 Underline the correct answer. Agnes Kovacs is:

a South African **b** Hungarian

3 Underline the correct answer. A *rival* is:

a an opponent **b** an antagonist **c** a competitor **d** an enemy

4 Sam always loved swimming. Is this true or false? ______________________________

5 Underline which one of the following Sam does not enjoy.

a snorkelling **b** black coffee **c** photography **d** friends

6 Sam was a *chronic asthmatic*. This means that Sam had:

a severe asthma attacks **b** continual asthma

c mild and infrequent asthma attacks **d** one near-fatal asthma attack

7 Why is it possible to call Sam an optimist? ______________________________

Writing skills

1 Why are the interviewer's questions in bold type? Underline two answers.

a to break up the small print

b because the interviewer is more important than his subject

c to distinguish between question and answer

2 Fill in the blanks. The first half of the interview deals with Sam's ______________________ life, the second deals with her ______________________ life.

3 Underline the correct answer. The interviewer asks about Sam's private life in a sports interview because he is:

a ill-mannered

b writing for professional sportspeople

c writing for general readers

4 Underline the correct answer. The third question begins with *so*. Why?

a because the interviewer made a mistake

b because the question clarifies the second answer

c because the interviewer was being sarcastic

5 The interviewer asks only short, simple questions. This technique allows the interviewee to answer as she wishes. The result of this technique is a sympathetic/negative interview. Underline the correct word.

6 A written version of an interview first recorded on audio or video tape is called a trans _ _ _ _ t.

7 Complete the following.

The questions are all very short because the interview is to tell us about Sam and not about the i _ _ _ _ _ _ _ _ _ _ .

8 Sam answered these questions in speech, not writing. Underline which of the following quotations from the interview proves this.

a I think I have two rivals. **b** I was dragged big time.

9 The answer to question 9 is an example of formal/colloquial language. Underline the correct word.

10 Why do you think the interview ends with the last question and not the second last?

____

Vocabulary

competitive	**attention**	**communicate**	**practise**	**practice**
serious	**favourite**	**fridge**	**asthmatic**	**valuable**

1 Break these long words into syllables to help with spelling.

2 Use the Look, Cover, Write, Check method with difficult words such as *asthmatic.*

3 Underline the homonyms *practise* and *practice* and study their use carefully (see Exercise 2 in 'Word study' below).

4 Underline the *'our'* in *favourite*. Beware of American spellcheck programs that do not use this spelling pattern. Australian English uses the English spelling system, not the American system.

Focus on punctuation

Commas

Commas help to make meaning clear.

Commas break sentences into reasonable lengths to allow a reader to draw breath and read intelligently. Commas therefore occur:

- after complete ideas, e.g.
  Not gasping for air, not even the slightest bit out of breath, Felix swam with calm strokes, and climbed from the quarry without once looking back.
- between words and their explanation or description, e.g.
  Claudia, the sister of Connie, earned her Bronze Lifesaving Award.

1 Add the missing commas according to the rules above and in Chapter 5.

a Builders are responsible for the laying of the foundations the erection of the frame the roofing of the frame the cladding of the walls and the fitting out of the house.

b The Eora who lived in the Sydney area when Europeans arrived suffered terribly from the smallpox brought by the newcomers.

c In one hectic day Peter went to school had cricket training fitted in his letterbox leafleting job debated with his school team and came home to do homework.

d The spy passed his information to his counterpart the undersecretary at the Rugovian Embassy.

e Jackie Chan an Australian from Canberra is an international film star.

2 Place commas for clear meaning and comfortable reading.

a On the other side of the creek near the apple gums a horse grazed contentedly.

b Mario my father's brother the man who runs the garden nursery is also a vintner.

c Dollarbirds the ones with small pale coin spots under their wings are migratory.

d Woodworkers carpenters joiners and furniture makers need good quality tools.

3 Which sentence is correctly punctuated? a, b, c or d? ____

a Mr Wilson's Ferrari the vintage wire-wheeled-red sports car is for sale.

b Mr Wilson's Ferrari, the vintage wire-wheeled-red sports car is for sale.

c Mr Wilson's Ferrari, the vintage wire-wheeled-red sports car, is for sale

d Mr Wilson's Ferrari, the vintage wire-wheeled-red sports car, is for sale.

Select a word

Choose words from the vocabulary list that mean the same as these words.

1 grave ____________________

2 precious ____________________

3 preferred ____________________

4 having a strong desire to win ____________________

5 convey a message ____________________

6 a medical or dental business ____________________

Grammar

Verbs and tenses

- Verbs do things, e.g. *cut, swim, fly, eat.*
- Actions occur at different times and so verbs have different times called tenses, e.g. *come* (present tense) *came* (past tense)

1 Underline any verbs in the following:

a chop **b** cheer **c** drive **d** memorise **e** happy

f read **g** chatter **h** red **i** improve **j** calculate

2 Write the past tense form:

a **i** eat __________ **ii** run __________ **iii** talk __________ **iv** speak __________

b Convert these sentences to past tense.

i They plan to go bowling. ____________________

ii We choose to avoid city traffic. ____________________

iii Michaela goes ice-skating on Saturday. ____________________

iv Triathletes run, swim and cycle long distances. ____________________

3 Convert these sentences to present tense.

a Dilip dived in the deep end. ____________________

b My brother loved that picture. ____________________

c Chloe drank all the lemonade. ____________________

d The tiger cub lapped water. ____________________

4 Is the *Moxiana* text of Chapter 5 written in present or past tense? ____________________

Word study

1 Insert words from the vocabulary list in the following.

a Tony Mundine was a very ______________ rugby player, never giving his opponents a chance to score if he could help it.

b Fouad loves soccer. It is his ______________ sport.

c To miss a train is not important, but to miss an exam is ______________.

d A coach may not ______________ with his team while the game is in progress.

2 **Homonyms** sound the same but have different meanings and are spelt differently, e.g. *practise* is a verb and *practice* is a noun.

An easy way to remember the difference here is to memorise:

- *Practise singing daily.*
- *'The Practice' is a cool TV show.*

Underline the correct alternative in the following.

a Please don't practice/practise your trumpet at night.

b Dr Phuoc's practice/practise is very busy.

c The practise/practice of checking age-identity cards limits underage drinking.

d He intends to practise/practice his violin concerto in the hall.

3 Circle the correct homonym in these sentences.

a Yesterday I red/read that an Australian invented the bionic ear.

b A wild storm set the herd/heard stampeding.

c When Mum rings/wrings out wet towels she takes off her wring/ring.

d Baking bread/bred is a long process.

e The old tree beside the creak/creek begins to creek/creak when the wind rises.

4 Write homonyms for these words. The homonyms must match the meanings on the right.

a	flee	_ _ _ _	a small biting insect
b	passed	_ _ _ _	times gone by
c	lone	_ _ _ _	something lent to someone else
d	hole	_ _ _ _ _	complete or entire

Evaluating other people's writing

Q *Why are you so late for this interview?*
A That's none of your business.
Q *Well, it is. I've got another interview to do after this. Well, let's get on with it. What's your favourite group?*
A My own, of course.
Q *Why did you call yourselves The Gongs?*
A You didn't read the promos we sent you. Did you?
Q *No. I haven't had time. Thought I'd do that after we talked. Sorry, mate.*
A Look, I'm not your mate and I haven't got time to waste. Read the stuff and then get back to my agent. I'm going to the studio now.

1 Does this interview get off to a promising start? Underline the correct alternative. Yes/No

2 Why is this so? Underline all possible reasons.

a interviewer unprepared

b interviewer rude

c interviewer asks uninformed questions

d interviewer inappropriately familiar

e interviewer asks irrelevant questions

3 Underline which of the following would have been a better opening question.

a I'm sorry you were delayed. Would you like to postpone the interview?

b I'm so glad you were able to get here. Was it the traffic that delayed you?

c I'm delighted to meet you. Could I offer you a coffee before we start?

4 Underline all correct answers. An interviewer should make the subject feel:

a appreciated **b** just part of his day's work **c** important

d relaxed **e** it is a big opportunity for the interviewer to make his name as an interviewer

Word usage

1 Insert words from the vocabulary list or other appropriate words.

a Pay ________________ as I dictate this message.

b Dolphins ________________ by sonar.

c The Koh-i-noor diamond is very ________________.

d An interview which discovers no new information is unpr _ _ _ _ _ _ _ _ .

2 Familiar speech is the language you use with your peers. It is too colloquial (everyday) and too personal for formal occasions. Read the following. Are they too familiar for the people to whom they are addressed? Underlined the correct alternative.

a To your school Principal: Knock it off, mate. You know I don't like detentions. Yes/No

b To your elderly neighbour: Can I give you a hand, Mr Jones? Yes/No

c To Sgt Smith telling you not to rollerblade in the mall: Sure, John. But lose the frown, it doesn't suit you. Yes/No

3 Write the correct formal term of address for each person from the list below.

Your Grace	Your Majesty	Mr/Madam (Ma'am)
President	Your Excellency	Sir/Madam (Ma'am)

a an ambassador ________________________ **b** a bishop ________________________

c a king or queen ________________________ **d** a prime minister ________________________

e a president ________________________

Quick think

Great verbs make great sentences! Underline the most interesting verb in each of the following matched pairs for inclusion in a piece of creative writing.

1 cry/sob **2** said/asserted **3** plummet/fall **4** wet/soak

5 demand/ask **6** slash/cut **7** devour/eat **8** walk/trudge

9 hit/pummelled **10** scold/yell at

Proofreading

Find six punctuation and four errors of verb tense in the following. Note: The first verb is correct.

Olivia leaned over the gate and looks down trinculo Road. There is nothing to be seen except an ancient truck and two men unloading fruit crates She sighs and idly swung on the gate while she contemplates whether to go looking for ming Lee in the library or down among the cd racks in Tony's Music house.

Idiom

Explain:

1 Keep an eye on it while I go and get help. ______________________

____

2 It rained cats and dogs all night. ______________________

____

Writing paragraphs and whole texts

1 You have won a half-hour interview with the sporting star of your choice. Think carefully about all you know of that star, then:

a Write four questions you would ask him/her during the interview.

____

____

____

____

b Write both your questions about what the star sees as his/her future after retirement and the star's answer to those questions.

____

____

c Sum up what the star has told you as one paragraph for readers.

____

____

____

____

____

2 Write an interview on your own paper between a reporter and Detective Sergeant Luke Smeaton about the Phantom. Use the facts in this report.

Phantom 'close to a mistake'

Police are confident they are closing in on Melbourne's notorious cat burglar, The Phantom, who has stolen $2 million in cash and jewellery in daring raids across the city's wealthy south-east.

The Phantom targets the Wheelers Hill area and has been blamed for up to 70 break-ins over the past four years, including seven in the past three weeks. He operates only at night and mostly in the cooler months, police said yesterday.

One of his latest victims, Fred Pearce, said he was visiting his dying mother-in-law in hospital when The Phantom struck.

'The last thing we need at this stage ... was for this sort of event to take place,' Mr Pearce said yesterday. 'It was just a total mess.'

Detective Sergeant Luke Smeaton said The Phantom probably watched people leaving their homes and then entered the rear of the property, climbing on to the roof and dropping through the ceiling.

He mainly steals items such as jewellery as well as cash.

Detective Smeaton said he thought The Phantom might be making the mistake of believing he's invincible.

'We believe that as it goes on, he becomes more complacent and more brazen, takes greater risks and to a certain extent obviously feels that he is reasonably invincible.'

Daily Telegraph

3 Your area is bushfire prone. Write the transcript of an interview you have with senior fire officer Clem De Groot about measures people should take to secure their homes in the event of a bushfire.

Chapter test

1 Circle the misspelling in this sentence.

Peter is practicing his skateboard moves.

2 Circle the correct tense of this sentence.

present tense past tense

The Marrickville Marauders were all out for 135 in just half an hour.

3 Which sentence is correctly punctuated? ____

a Sami Selena's little sister, is in hospital

b Sami, Selena's little sister is in hospital.

c Sami, Selena's little sister, is in hospital.

d Sami, Selena's little sister, is in hospital

CHAPTER 7

Play script

STRUCTURE

- *scripts are written in **acts** (sections of plot) and scenes (separate settings for parts of that act's activity)*
- *everything the audience knows at the end is conveyed by the dialogue they hear and the actions and sets they see*

title of play and act and scene details

directions for set designer and director, who build stage scenery and place actors in stage

dialogue/ actors' lines

directions for actor's speech style

directions for actor movement so audience can see what Selena is showing Penny

directions for actor movement

directions to sound effects technician

Bits of Metal

Act III, Scene II

Scene: A high school quadrangle in inner Sydney. Two brick walls meet right of centre at the rear of the stage. The left wall is blind and has a basketball hoop fixed high just beyond mid-point. The right wall has a row of windows above head height and a set of steps at the right front of the stage leading to double doors in the wall. One door is ajar.

Three girls are talking and desultorily shooting goals. Two girls, Penny Stathakis and Selena Turkogolou, are deep in conversation on the step. Both are dark haired. Penny is stocky and Selena thin.

Penny: *(raising her head)* ... and Grandma just cried and cried. Mum couldn't stop her. And Dad was yelling and crying at the same time. Aunty Maria kept butting in and saying that maybe it wasn't true and maybe he was just taken prisoner.

Selena: What did you do?

Penny: I never knew Georgiou. He was just one of the cousins in Mum's photo album. Grandma thought he was special 'cause he was the first grandson and she always had a picture of him on the mantelpiece. It was a picture taken at some festival in Nicosia and he's wearing Greek clothes. Anyway, I wasn't crying or anything but I felt kind of ... sick. Somehow everything's going to change now, I think. My father said Mum can't get her hair done at your shop any more.

Selena: *(slowly)* When this Cyprus business started my uncle gave me this badge to wear *(holds up a red disc about 5 centimetres across and carrying a white crescent moon imprinted on it)*. It's the same as the Turkish flag. He said I had to wear it to honour all the family who are in the war. I didn't want to upset him so I said yes and put it in my pocket but I felt just like you ... sort of sick. I feel really mixed up about everything. I didn't say anything to you about it because I didn't know how you felt about this horrible Greek–Turk Cyprus thing.

Penny: *(vehemently)* I hate it!

Selena: So do I. I'm frightened everything's going to be different now.

Penny: Well, we just can't let it be different. I'm sorry Georgiou's dead and I'm sorry Grandma's upset but that happened in Cyprus. The war's in Cyprus, not over here, not in Sydney. It's not my war. And it's not your war either. *(She pulls a chain holding an Orthodox cross from around her neck.)* This is what Grandma gave me to wear when the war started. Give me that badge, Selena.

Selena: *(handing it over)* What for? You've broken that chain. Won't your Grandma be mad at you for that?

Penny: She's not going to know. Come on, get up, we've got something to do.

(She moves to centre stage and flings both objects off stage into a water tub below audience eye level. Two distinct splashes are heard.)

Let Mrs Baker's precious goldfish wear these wretched bits of metal. God, how I hate those fish! Wouldn't you think a high school principal would have a more grown-up hobby than goldfish!

Selena: Maybe the fish'll choke on them, the badge and cross I mean.

Penny: Better than us choking on all that 'old enemy' stuff anyway. Let's see if we can challenge Connie Rivas to a first-to-five shoot before maths. *(Linking arms they move off to join the group about the basketball hoop, Selena scooping up a stray ball as they go.)*

(Extract from a work in progress)

LANGUAGE FEATURES

script writing is designed to present a slice of life on stage, so the language:

- *must be true to life*
- *must be detailed so that the audience even knows what the characters remember and think*

short informative statements for the benefit of directors and actors

longer conversational sentences

colloquial language

details for audience's benefit

direct statements and questions to link both characters to each other and the action

informal sentence style

Comprehension

1 Underline the correct answer. What is the news about cousin Georgiou?

a He has attended a festival in Nicosia. **b** He is missing.

c He is dead. **d** He is the first grandson.

2 Why is Penny's grandmother so upset? ______________________________

3 Selena is of Greek Cypriot ancestry. Is this true or false? ______________________________

4 Explain why Penny's mother is forbidden by her husband to go to her usual hairdresser. ______________

____

5 Underline the correct answer. The badge and cross have been given to the girls as:

a gifts **b** symbols of their country of origin **c** an identification with battle lines in a war

6 What are the girls afraid will change as a result of the war? ______________________________

____

7 Underline two answers. Penny threw the badge and cross into the pond:

a to spite their families **b** to demonstrate friendship

c to prevent change **d** to kill the goldfish

e to signify that they will not let the past control their lives

f to show they do not care about what is happening in Cyprus

8 The scene closes on a note of:

a fear **b** antagonism **c** friendship **d** unhappiness

9 The playwright has included a reference to the Principal's goldfish hobby as:

a pointless comment **b** light relief **c** an example of meanness

Writing skills

1 Underline the correct answer. The stage directions come before the actual dialogue to:

a avoid dialogue confusion **b** direct the stage set-up for the action

c permit a reader to understand the setting

2 Underline the correct answer. For whom have the scene setting directions been written?

a director **b** critics **c** actors **d** audience **e** set designer **f** producer

3 Underline the correct answer. For whom have the scene setting directions been written?

a The play is currently being performed. **b** The playwright has not finished writing the script.

c The play is currently being rehearsed.

4 What do the three dots (ellipsis) at the beginning of Penny's first sentence indicate? ______________

____

5 List two things covered by stage directions in this script. (Consider directions throughout the text.)

____

6 Why must Selena show the badge to the audience? ______________________________

7 What is the high point of this scene? ____________________

8 In dramatic terms what is this high point of a scene called? ____________________

9 What line in the scene breaks the tension built up to the climax? ____________________

____

10 Underline the most precise answer. The scene ends at the basketball hoop and not at the pond to:

a restore a sense of normality **b** offer a suggestion of hope

c demonstrate the absence of enmity between the girls

Vocabulary

rehearsal	direction	actor	illuminate	craft
instruction	light	skill	practice	dialogue

1 Think about how these words relate to drama production.

2 Practise noun/verb groupings using words in the vocabulary list, e.g. *rehearse/rehearsal, act/actor.* Say these words groupings aloud to fix them in your mind. This will allow you to master twenty words in this chapter.

3 Use the Look, Cover, Write, Check method to learn their spellings.

Focus on punctuation

Inverted commas

Inverted commas enclose the actual words spoken by someone and any end punctuation attached. You must start a new paragraph each time a new speaker talks, e.g.

'Who scratched my new CD?' yelled Tony.

Peter shouted back, 'Well, it wasn't me!'

'Well it certainly wasn't me!' retorted Tony.

Note: Double inverted commas may be used instead of single inverted commas. In this book single inverted commas are used.

Add the inverted commas.

1 What's the budget for this documentary? the producer asked.

2 We're looking for an actor to play the dying pioneer, said the casting director.

3 If you can't be available for six months you can't audition, Peter announced.

4 The director shouted, Everyone back on set immediately!

5 Where is the shield to go with this sword? the props manager asked.

6 Hey Jack, the cameraman called. Look to the camera, please.

Select a word

Write words that mean the same as the following.

1 stage furniture: _ _ _

2 text of play: _ _ _ _ _ _

3 writer of play: _ _ _ _ _ _ _ _ _ _ _

4 an actor's part in play: _ _ _ _

5 building to stage a play: _ _ _ _ _ _ _

6 building to screen a film: _ _ _ _ _ _

Grammar

Verbs, continuous tenses

Verbs can refer to action currently happening, e.g.

- *I am going to rehearsal now.* **Present continuous tense**
- *They were going to the theatre yesterday.* **Past continuous tense**
- *You will be studying Shakespeare in Year 11.* **Future continuous tense**

1 Change the underlined verbs to the continuous form indicated.

a They will be going to the One Direction concert. (Past continuous) ____________________

b Movie prices are getting dearer, concert tickets are getting dearer, no one is happy. (Past continuous)

____

c Sam and Eddy were planning to go to a drama workshop in their holidays. (Present continuous)

____

d Year 7 are going to see a production of *The Hobbit.* (Future continuous) ____________________

____

2 Make each underlined verb continuous in the same tense.

a The local drama group staged the musical *Cats.* __________

b Our school will hold a talent quest next week. __________

c Our family goes to the summer Opera in the Park series. __________

d The old Odeon cinema was demolished. __________

Word study

Words that have the same meaning are called **synonyms**, e.g. *cold* and *chill.*

1 Match these words from the vocabulary list words with their synonyms, also from the vocabulary list.

a rehearsal ______________ **b** instruction ______________

c craft ______________ **d** light ______________

2 Write the following as verbs.

a practice ______________ **b** direction ______________

c rehearsal ______________ **d** instruction ______________

3 Insert appropriate words from the vocabulary list.

a In Sydney stage __________ can be learned at NIDA.

b The theatre was in darkness but the stage was __________d.

c Smithy had rap-dancing __________ to improve his act for the Sydney Rock Festival.

4 These are all people associated with theatre and film. Complete their names.

a one who edits a film clip: e _ _ _ _ _ r

b writer of a film script: s _ _ _ _ tw _ _ _ _ r

c one directing actors in their work: d _ _ _ _ t _ r

d one who oversees the production of the work: p _ _ d _ _ _ r

e one who takes the film shots: c _ _ _ r _ m _ n

Evaluating other people's writing

The note

Charlie: Well, you've just got to trust me. I'm the only chance you've got.

Peter: I don't like you. You lied to me. How can I trust you?

Simon: 'Cause you can't trust him. Remember how he dobbed you in to old Carney.

Charlie: I didn't, you rotten little sneak. That was you!

Peter: Shut up, both of you. I don't care about Carney. It's what I'm going to do about this that's got to be sorted out. How can I get that note back before she reads it?

Which of the following essential elements are missing from this script?

1 title

2 act or scene number

3 stage directions for set

4 dialogue

5 directions for actors

6 credits

Word usage

1 Underline the correct word.

a A successful musician practises/practices every day.

b Everyone accept/except Sonja was there on opening night.

c The principle/principal, Mrs Joan Armstrong, will attend the Rock Festival.

d Maria's writing is illegible/eligible so her script will be rejected.

2 Underline the correct verb form

a Peter did/done his homework.

b Salim and Ah Kee might of/might have caught a later bus.

c Connie could of/could have played that role well.

d Spyros should have/should of learned his lines.

3 Correct the underlined words in this text:

That actor <u>might of</u> been hurt when he came <u>of</u> his horse. He could <u>have fell</u> on a rock and <u>broke</u> a bone or got caught with his foot <u>hanged</u> in a stirrup.

a ______________________ **b** ______________________ **c** ______________________

d ______________________ **e** ______________________

Quick think

The following all relate to the interior of a theatre.

1 Underline the correct answer. Those who watch a production are:

a spectators **b** a congregation **c** an audience

2 Fill in the blanks in the following:

a A try-out for a role is an au _ _ _ ion.

b An actor's clothing is his/her c _ _ _ _ _ e.

c Random noises deliberately made on stage are s _ _ _ _ e _ _ _ _ _ s.

d One who organises and pays for a drama production is a p _ _ _ _ _ _ r.

e One who guides the actors, set, costume and make-up artists is a d _ _ _ _ _ _ r.

Proofreading

Correct the following for paragraphs ([), punctuation and spelling.

William shakespeare rote plays in the sixteent centry the teacher told his class he wrote comedys, tradgedies and history plays. Was he an Australian vincent wanted to now. No, he was an englishman replied mr theodosiou.

Idiom

Explain:

1 'Oh, Mum. That's looking for a needle in a haystack,' Paul said when asked to find a missing sock.

____

2 'Oh, put a sock in it, mate,' Nyugen said to his brother, who was chattering constantly. __________

____

Writing paragraphs and whole texts

1 Write directions for the characters in 'The note' in the section 'Evaluating other people's writing'. Include dress, appearance, personality and stage position at the beginning of the extract. Write in complete sentences.

Charlie ______________________________

____

Simon ______________________________

____

Peter ______________________________

____

2 Describe the set you would use for this scene. Make it as realistic as possible but still able to be set up in five minutes by three people (so not too big, not too heavy and certainly not too expensive to make).

____

____

____

____

____

____

____

3 Using the following facts write a script for an encounter at a bus stop. Include all stage directions (for set, lighting, movement and dialogue).

Facts: a dark wet afternoon, late bus, crowded bus stop, students from two different schools, a minor accident, a possible romance

Don't forget that each actor's dialogue starts on a new line.

4 Write clear directions for playing the character of an old man who uses a walking stick and is hard of hearing. Consider the way he would walk (confidently? comfortably? easily? quickly?) and what he might do with his hands to help him hear better.

Chapter test

1 Circle the word that means the same as the underlined word.

regulations   instructions   advice   map

Ben's <u>directions</u> were that people should meet at four o'clock on the bridge.

2 Rewrite this sentence in past continuous tense.

He climbed the old walnut tree.

3 Which sentence is correctly punctuated? ______

a Where are you going? she asked.

b 'Where are you going' she asked.

c 'Where are you going?' she asked

d 'Where are you going?' she asked.

CHAPTER 8

Book jacket

STRUCTURE

cover

- *front—details of title and author*
- *spine—details of title, author and publisher*
- *back—blurb*

- *publication details*
- *illustrator details*
- *price details*
- *ISBN details*

LANGUAGE FEATURES

succinct (brief, meaningful) title

type chosen for subject and for target reader relevance

explanatory subtitle

bold attention: grabbing key phrases in blurb

blurb text:

- *introduction—direct approach to prospective readers*
- *body—gruesome description to attract horror story addicts*
- *conclusion—involves reader choice*

Comprehension

1 What is the subtitle of this book? ______________________________

2 Name the author and cover illustrator. ________________ ________________

3 Name the publisher of this book. ______________________________

4 What is the recommended retail price of this book? ______________________________

5 The abbreviation ISBN stands for Inter__________al St__________d B________k N________r.

6 What is this book about? Give at least two reasons for your answer. ______________________________

____

7 This book involves the reader in an unusual way. How? ______________________________

____

8 Why is the title printed on the spine of the book when it is already on the cover? ______________

____

Writing skills

1 How does the title suggest what kind of story is in this book? ______________________

____

2 Underline the correct answers. The print style of the title suggests which of the following?
a youth **b** maturity **c** adulthood **d** fear **e** haste **f** humour

3 What elements of the front cover suggest fear and supernatural events? ______________

____

4 List three grim visual elements in the back cover illustration. ______________________

____

5 Explain why the illustrator included headstones in his cover design. ______________

6 The 'blurb' is written in the second person (you). Why? ______________________

____

7 Underline the correct answer. Three pieces of text are highlighted in the 'blurb'. Why?
a to catch your attention **b** to emphasise parts of the book **c** to accentuate horror

8 What will the skeleton be doing if it is 'stalking' you and will you know it is doing so? Answer in one sentence. ____

____

9 Who or what does the logo on the back cover represent? ______________________

Vocabulary

horror	**terror**	**panic**	**fright**	**ghost**
horrible	**terrible**	**supernatural**	**frightful**	**ghostly**

Common spelling patterns at the ends of words include *~ight* and *~ible*. Learn these and you will be halfway to spelling lots of other words that end in these patterns.

Learn matching nouns and adjectives together. It makes spelling much easier. Don't forget the Look, Cover, Write, Check method.

Focus on punctuation

Inverted commas

Inverted commas enclose titles of books, films, newspapers etc., e.g.
My favourite book is Morris Gleitzman's 'Two Weeks with The Queen'.

However, if you are typing, or if the material is published (e.g. this book), you use italics for these titles.

Inverted commas also enclose quotations, e.g.
Queen Victoria's most famous comment was: 'We are not amused.'

Insert inverted commas in the following. You may use single or double inverted commas.

1 Have you seen Happy Feet yet?

2 It was Queen Marie Antoinette who said of the starving citizens of Paris Why don't they eat cake?

3 Play School is a popular Australian TV production for preschoolers.

4 Our Maths teacher's favourite saying is See what fun algebra can be.

5 Australian sayings such as flat out like a lizard drinking are old-fashioned now.

6 If a job's worth doing, it's worth doing well his father told him.

Select a word

1 Four synonyms for *ghost* are:

a sp _ _ _ _ e

b po _ _ _ _ g _ _ st

c sp _ _ _ t

d ph _ _ t _ m

2 Four synonyms for *fear* are:

a f _ _ ght

b t _ _ _ _ r

c d _ _ _ d

d p _ _ _ c

Grammar

Verbs, future tenses

Verbs can include two or more words. One is the **main** verb; the others are **auxiliary** or **helping** verbs. A **finite** or **complete** verb includes both main and auxiliary verbs, e.g.

- *I ate my lunch.* Finite verb
- *I have eaten my lunch.* Finite verb including auxiliary *have*
- *I will have eaten my lunch before lunchtime.* Finite verb including auxiliaries *will* and *have*

Future tense is the verb form used when the action is happening in the future, e.g.

- *He will finish school in May.* **Simple future tense**
- *Shall I catch the first or the second bus?* **Simple future tense**
- *I will have finished high school by the time I am eighteen.* **Future perfect tense**
- *She will be meeting us at four.* **Future continuous tense**

1 Underline the complete (finite) verb in the future tense.

a You will need a coat in the snow tomorrow.

b Will they be taking Year 7 on that excursion?

c Where will you be tomorrow night?

d She will have read that whole book by tonight.

e We will have seen all Sydney has to offer within a week.

2 Change to simple future tense.

a I went to the Lady Gaga concert. ______________________________

b They are here promptly. ______________________________

3 Change to future perfect tense.

a I will go at six o'clock. ______________________________

b You should do your homework on Saturday. ______________________________

4 Change to future continuous tense.

a We will swim this afternoon. ______________________________

b They went to Dragon Rock. ______________________________

c Michael plays the flute. ______________________________

5 Write the tense of the underlined verbs.

a They *have been singing* for two hours. ______________________________

b Ghosts *will not appear* before dark. ______________________________

c After dark, if you listen, the owls *will be hooting*. ______________________________

d *Shall* I *do* that for you? ______________________________

Word study

1 Choose words from the vocabulary list that mean the same as these words.

a not natural ____________________ **b** sudden unreasoning fear ____________________

c extreme fear ____________________ **d** intense revulsion and fear ____________________

2 Insert these words appropriately in the following.

blurb, title, style, layout

a The ________ of the book was 'Wild Cat Falling'.

b Morris Gleitzman's writing ________ is humorous.

c After reading the ________ on the back I decided to borrow the book.

d With knights, dragons, trolls and lakes of fire the ________ of this book jacket was just too crowded.

3 Underline the answer that is best described by these words.

a horrible: a giant, slimy eel/a shark

b frightful: an ugly person/an avenging dragon

c terrible: an ogre/a chihuahua

4 The words *horrible* and *terrible* are often used carelessly when other words would be more accurate. Replace these words in the following with words from the list below. Use each word only once.

disruptive, illegible, stern, difficult

a I've had a terrible day. ____________________

b Mrs Banks is a horrible teacher. ____________________

c That's horrible writing for an assessment essay. ____________________

d Max's behaviour in class is terrible. ____________________

5 Complete these *~ight* and *~ible* words.

a The Great Australian _ ight

b power and strength: _ ight

c unfortunate situation: _ _ ight

d the act of flying: _ _ ight

e not loose-fitting: _ ight

f can be eaten: e _ ible

g can happen: p _ _ _ ible

h reasonable: s _ _ _ ible

i can be seen: v _ _ ible

j can be read: l _ _ ible

Word usage

<u>Funny</u> characters are everywhere. <u>Ever fearless</u> spacemen battle bad monsters in a red landscape <u>where nothing grows</u>. Struggling <u>first human settlers</u> crouch in <u>deep holes made by meteors</u> and wait to be <u>eaten</u> by the <u>big</u> worm <u>that makes tunnels</u>.

*Thar, <u>of noble rank and son of the King of Kor</u>, who was assassinated, has to fight <u>a one-to-one fight</u> with the Earl of Ido to <u>get back</u> his principality and his <u>newly married wife</u>.

This is a jacket 'blurb' for a science fiction novel called *Alpha Centauri*. It could be much shorter and more interesting with careful editing.

1 Underline the best substitute for:

a funny: humorous, bizarre, comic, strange

b ever fearless: brave, gallant, intrepid, courageous

2 Write one word for:

a where nothing grows b ______________________

b first human settlers p ______________________

c deep holes made by meteors c ______________________

d that makes tunnels t ______________________

e one-to-one fight d ______________________

f get back r ______________________

g newly married wife b ______________________

3 Write <u>stronger</u> words for:

a bad e _ _ l **b** eaten d _ _ _ _ _ _ d **c** big g _ _ _ t

4 Rewrite the sentence marked* so that it is shorter and simpler yet keeps the same meaning.

____

____

Quick think

1 Name your murder:

a to kill yourself s ______________________

b to kill someone else h ______________________

c to kill your brother f ______________________

d to kill a baby i ______________________

e to kill a race g ______________________

2 What suffix indicates a murder? ______________________

3 Ghosts traditionally move lightly. Underline any verb in the following that would not be appropriate to a ghostly movement.

a glide **b** waft **c** charge **d** drift **e** slip **f** hover **g** canter

4 Insert the missing letters. Ghosts are tr _ _ _ _ _ _ _ _ t (can be seen through) but not in _ _ _ _ _ le (not able to be seen).

Proofreading

Rewrite the following in **formal** language. It is to be used as an official accident report. In its present state it is unsuitable for its purpose.

> This bloke came screaming down the hill, ran the lights and collected the old guy's car that was coming the other way. I reckon it was all his fault, the bloke in the red car that shot through the lights, I mean.

____

____

____

Idiom

Explain:

1 He was <u>up the creek without a paddle</u> when it came to maths. ______________________

____

2 One black chook in a shed of white chooks is <u>the exception that proves the rule</u>. ______________________

____

Writing paragraphs and whole texts

1 Print these book titles in a style that will emphasise their subjects.

a The Ghoul (a ghost story) ______________________

b Dragon Tower (a murder mystery) ______________________

2 Write an appropriate subtitle for these books.

a The Night Visitor ______________________

b Vengeance of the Trolls ______________________

3 On these book spines arrange the following information. Use two different styles and layouts (setting out).

A

Author: MJ Milanos

Title: Shadows

Publisher: Shield Press

Logo

B

Author: Xu Ning

Title: Murder at the City Wall

Publisher: White Cross Books

Logo

4 Write a 'blurb' for the back of your favourite novel on your own paper. Make sure you include the information about the following: plot (what happens), main characters, and any exciting or humorous incident that would attract prospective readers.

____

____

____

____

____

____

____

____

____

5 Explain what the following are.

a an autobiography ______________________

b a biography ______________________

c a work of fiction ______________________

d a ship's logbook ______________________

e a journal ______________________

6 The first sentence of a story is crucial to its success. It can be very short or quite long but it has to grab the reader's interest.

a Write a dramatic action-based first sentence for *The Ghoul* (a ghost story).

____

____

b Write an atmospheric first sentence describing the Dragon Tower where a young prince is reputed to have been foully murdered. Other deaths are going to occur in this tower.

____

____

Chapter test

1 Which word is misspelt?

a terrible **b** frightfull **c** supernatural **d** panic

2 Write the correct form of the verb *to be* in the space.

If he wins this last race he ____________ Age Champion of the 14 Years – Boys.

3 Which sentence is correctly punctuated? __

a My grandfather's favourite exclamation is By George.

b My grandfather's favourite exclamation is, By George!

c My grandfather's favourite exclamation is By George!

d My grandfather's favourite exclamation is 'By George!'

CHAPTER 9

Instructions

STRUCTURE

LANGUAGE FEATURES

diagram (introduction)

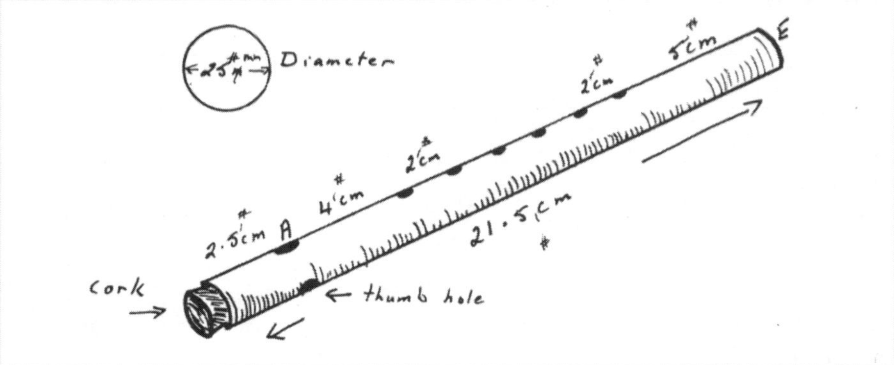

HOW TO MAKE AND PLAY A FLUTE

list of materials required for task →

Materials: one rigid tube 25 mm in diameter, e.g. bamboo, PVC pipe, electrical conduit
one cork to fit tube
measuring rule and pencil
saw
drill with 50 mm bit
round file

← *technical terms (**jargon**) appropriate to task*

← *simple facts, no verbs listed for ticking off*

Method:

1. Cut tube to length.
2. Insert cork in one end.
3. Draw a straight line the length of your tube.
4. From the cork end measure 2.5 cm along the pencil line and mark that spot.
5. Drill a hole at that point (being careful to pierce only one side of the tube).
6. Using the file shape this hole into an oval about 1 cm wide and centred on the pencilled line. This is the mouthpiece (A).
7. Beginning 5 cm from the end of the tube (E) mark a spot for each finger hole 2 cm apart as in the diagram. Take care to mark accurately along the pencilled line and in line with the centre of the mouthpiece (A).
8. Drill holes at each marked spot. (Note that these holes correspond to the musical scale of C.)
9. Turn the tube over and drill a thumb hole exactly under the mouthpiece.
10. File rough edges of all holes smooth.

chronological numbered list of manufacturing steps →

← *verbs in **imperative mood** (written as orders)*

← *all statements, no questions*

← *very few adjectives except where necessary to define fact*

← *explanatory phrases in brackets*

conclusion →

To play: Hold the flute with both hands with the left thumb covering thumb hole and the fingers closing all holes except the note you wish to play. Blow across the mouthpiece. Create melodies by stopping various holes in sequence as you blow.

← *short, precise sentences*

Comprehension

1 This flute could be made from a length of garden hose. Is this true or false? ____________

2 What part of the drill is the 'bit'? ____________

3 Underline the correct answer. In an orchestra this flute would belong among the:

a stringed instruments **b** brass instruments **c** wind instruments **d** percussion instruments

4 How is the saw used in the making of the flute? ____________

____

5 The mouthpiece is oval in shape. Underline which of the following does not share the same shape.

a an Australian Rules football field **b** an ellipse

c an egg **d** a discus

6 Explain why one end of the flute is closed with a cork. ____________

____

7 The reference to the musical scale of C suggests that the holes along the length of the flute are related to production of:

a sound **b** air **c** musical sound ____________

8 Which of these would be suitable tubing for making a flute?

a a drinking straw **b** a wooden curtain rod **c** a length of copper pipe ____________

Writing skills

1 Underline the correct answer. The diagram precedes the written directions:

a for interest attraction **b** for ease of reference **c** nowhere else to put it

2 Why are the materials listed rather than written in a paragraph? ____________

____

3 The list is compiled in random order. Is this true or false? ____________

4 Verbs in instructions are always written in the imperative mood. These verbs do not invite or ask; they tell. From the 'Method' section write down the first two examples of verbs in the imperative mood.

____________ ____________

5 Replace these words in the passage with appropriate alternatives. Some letters have been provided as clues.

a rigid: _ _ _ ff **b** spacing: _ _ ps **c** accurately: pr _ _ _ _ _ ly **d** correspond to: _ _ _ ch

6 Explain the order in which the Method activities have been written.

____

7 What synonym is used for *closing* in the last paragraph? ____________

8 The use of a synonym instead of the same word again adds ____________ to your writing. Underline any of the following words that would correctly fill the blank in the previous sentence.

a interest **b** variety **c** confusion

d obscurity **e** clarity

9 The phrase *in sequence* means ____________ after ____________ other.

10 A writer of instructions would not use which of these?

a dialogue **b** colourfully descriptive language **c** facts
d long paragraphs **e** discussion **f** short sentences **g** complex terminology

Vocabulary

improvise	**harmonise**	**analyse**	**visualise**	**minimise**
orchestrate	**manipulate**	**capitulate**	**prevaricate**	**estimate**

Learn these as two groups: an *~ise* group (apart from *analyse*) and an *~ate* group. A common pattern always helps the memory. Note: Australian English uses *~ise*. The American spelling *~ize* is not used here.

Focus on punctuation

Apostrophe of abbreviation

Words can be shortened by inserting an apostrophe in place of the omitted letter.

1 Write the abbreviated forms of these words.

a will not ____________ **b** could not ____________ **c** would not ____________
d could have ____________ **e** might have ____________ **f** should have ____________

2 Abbreviate the underlined words using an apostrophe, e.g.

It is my book. It's my book.

a It is my party and I will cry if I want to. ____________ ____________
b They cannot go with us. ____________
c Unless you are here we will not leave. ____________ ____________
d Jim will be MC at the social on Friday. ____________
e Where is the box of CDs I left on the stage? ____________

3 Insert the apostrophes.

I wouldnt have minded if hed asked me. He couldve borrowed all my gear and it wouldnt have worried me a bit. But to take it without asking, thats too much. Its plain bad manners as far as Im concerned.

4 Write the correct abbreviated words to replace these underlined errors.

Louis Xiaou and Eddie might of won the three-legged race if they could of stood up when they fell over. They were in the lead then but couldnt' get up no matter how they tried. Their legs just wouldnt cooperate.

____

Select a word

Find words in the list that mean:

1 surrender ____________ **2** imagine ____________
3 make do ____________ **4** guess ____________
5 arrange ____________ **6** shrink ____________

Grammar

Subject and verb agreement

All verbs must agree with their subject. That is, if the subject is singular (one person, one thing etc.) the verb will have a singular form, e.g.
John is going to the beach.
Sing. subj. Sing. verb

If the subject is plural (more than one) the verb will have a plural form, e.g.
The girls are going abseiling.
Pl. subj Pl. verb

Note: collective nouns—e.g. *flock, crew*—are followed by singular verbs, e.g.
The crew was wet and exhausted.
Coll. noun Sing. verb

1 Underline the correct verb form.

a John and his mate has/have gone swimming.

b The audience was/were rapt.

c Classes is/are inclined to drowse in the afternoon.

d David and his guitar are/is never separated.

e The team are/is to contest the Grand Finals.

2 Write a correct form of the verb in brackets on the line following.

a The horses (to race) ______________ around the paddock yesterday afternoon.

b Five sprinters (to compete) ______________ in the 100 metres sprint tomorrow.

c Each girl (to swallow) ______________ her medicine when it was administered.

d All of them must (to eat) ______________ their dinner by now.

e The cat (to lap) ______________ its milk while the canary sings.

f The orchestra (to tune) ______________ its instruments before the concert began.

g Right now the kangaroo mob (to laze) ______________ in the shade.

h A herd of wildebeest in full charge (to be) ______________ a fearsome sight.

i We saw a shoal of sardines (to swirl) ______________ in a great ball under our boat.

j A tribe of chimpanzees (to be) ______________ very close knit.

Word study

1 Complete these sentences with words from the vocabulary list.

a The lead singer encouraged his group to ______________ rather than drown each other out.

b Napoleon ______________d to Wellington at the Battle of Waterloo.

c With a stick and a tin can any baby can ______________ a toy drum.

d A student can only ______________ the time it will take to complete an assignment.

e 'If I close my eyes I can ______________ myself on stage wowing them at the Sydney Entertainment Centre,' Lisa confided to her friend.

f To ______________ hearing loss many rock musicians wear ear plugs.

g The bandmaster has promised to ______________ that sound track for our band.

h For a juggler to ______________ six balls in the air at once, great skill is required.

i Don't ______________, do it now!

j When we ______________ these figures we'll know whether the concert made a profit.

2 If two words mean the opposite of each other they are called **antonyms**, e.g. *good/bad*. Write the antonyms of these words.

a small ______________________ **b** wide ______________________
c mountain ______________________ **d** day ______________________
e deciduous ______________________ **f** fresh ______________________
g wealthy ______________________ **h** industrious ______________________

3 Prefixes are attached to the beginning of a word, e.g. *<u>un</u>likely*, *<u>anti</u>social*. Use the prefix *un~* or the prefix *anti~* to create antonyms from these words.

a usual ______________________ **b** matter ______________________
c sympathetic ______________________ **d** imaginative ______________________
e climax ______________________ **f** interested ______________________
g realistic ______________________ **h** biotic ______________________

Word usage

Read these two passages aloud. They are both about the same incident.

A: Formal version

The first vehicle, a red sports car, approached the traffic lights at the intersection of Cooma and Rossi Streets at high speed. Witnesses said that it appeared the driver did not see the truck laden with gravel entering the intersection from his right. The impact of the resulting collision caused the truck to slew wildly. It then overturned spilling its load over the sports car which had been hurled into the telegraph pole on the corner occupied by Martin's Toy Store. The truck driver was shaken but uninjured. The driver of the sports car died at the instant of impact.

B: Informal version

It was a real mess, gravel all over the place. The little car, one of those sports jobs with wire wheels, <u>was wrapped around the pole</u> and the gravel from the truck was all over it. <u>It, the red car, the sporty one</u>, came flying down the hill as if there were no tomorrow. <u>It didn't have a chance of stopping—even if he saw the truck, which I don't think he did</u>.

1 Informal language is characterised by the following characteristics. Match them to the underlined examples in passage B.

a colourful colloquial words and images ______________________

b lack of precision ______________________

c statements immediately followed by modifications or conditions ______________________

____

2 From passage A find the formal version of these extracts from passage B.

a The little car, one of those sports jobs ______________________

b Flying down the hill like there was no tomorrow ______________________

3 Because informal language is usually unplanned, important information is often left out. List three facts included in passage A which have been left out of passage B.

a ______________________________

b ______________________________

c ______________________________

Quick think

1 Underline the best formal version of the following.

a I'll do my darndest to be there on the dot.

- **i** I will try very hard to be punctual.
- **ii** I'll try very hard to be there on the dot.

b Get a wriggle on or you'll be late.

- **i** Hurry up or you'll be late.
- **ii** Hurry or you will be late.

c No way! I'm not doing that—not for love nor money.

- **i** No way! I will not do that for anything.
- **ii** Certainly not! Nothing would persuade me to do that.

2 Complete these well-known colloquial descriptions.

a as pretty as a ______________ **b** as ugly as ______________

c as bright as a ______________ **d** as quick as a ______________

e as skinny as a ______________

3 Fill in the blanks. Because they are well known and overused the colloquial descriptions above are unsuitable for formal writing; they are called cl _ ch _ s.

Proofreading

Underline and correct any incorrect homonyms, e.g. *mail/male*. Write the correct words below.

Ferry tails about the likes of Jack and his pale of water can be red in any child's story book. You can also reed biblical storeys like that of the baby Moses floating in his read basket among the reeds of the Nile River.

____

____

Idiom

Explain:

1 I wouldn't say thank you for it. ______________________________

____

2 'Give us a break,' Kai groaned when he was given three maths exercises for homework. ______________

____

Writing paragraphs and whole texts

1 The information below is a set of instructions for making a caramel self-saucing pudding. (It works!) Place the instructions in the correct order. Remember sequence.

___ **a** Bake in moderate oven till pudding rises and surface cracks (approx. 35 mins).

___ **b** Place all ingredients in an ovenproof bowl:

c $1\frac{1}{2}$ cups self-raising flour
$\frac{2}{3}$ cup sugar
1 large tablespoon butter/margarine
1 egg
1 cup milk (more if mixture too dry)

___ **d** Beat to a smooth consistency.

___ **e** Shake 1 cup brown sugar over the top of the mixture. Do not mix in.

___ **f** Pour 2 cups cold water over all.

2 Read the following passage. Using the information contained, write clear numbered instructions for raising a newborn orphan kitten.

Penny arrived home with the latest addition to the menagerie, a tiny still-blind kitten rescued from the dump. Too small to maintain its own body temperature, Ginger Whinge had to be kept wrapped in a piece of blanket in Penny's jacket pocket where she could share Penny's warmth.

Every two hours night and day Penny fed the tiny creature. She held it in her lap on its side and bottle-fed it a formula mix given by the vet, who also provided the minuscule bottle and teat. At the end of each feeding session, Penny, as surrogate mother, had to wipe the kitten's rear end with a warm, damp washer to ensure it relieved itself regularly and cleanly. This its own mother would have done by licking.

After a week its eyes opened and the kitten grew curious. It now needed play time under supervision to allow it to explore its world without hurting itself or getting stuck somewhere. It also needed much more to drink and things to chew on to help its teeth come through. By five weeks it was sleeping through the night, lapping milk from a saucer and needed only an odd bottle, more for the sake of comfort and affection than from hunger.

3 Following these instructions draw the mystery picture and then complete the sentence below.

1 Draw a horizontal line 10 cm long.

2 Draw a semicircle with a radius of 2 cm in the middle of the top side of the line.

3 On the diameter of the semicircle draw two upside-down letters 'U' and add one large black dot in the top of each.

4 On the top of the semicircle draw a single small vertical curly line.

5 Attach a letter 'C' to the outside of the semicircle on the left just above the horizontal line, and attach another to match on the right, only in reverse form.

6 Draw two letters 'm' joined together 1 cm inside each end of the horizontal line.

I wish / _ / _ _ _ _ / t _ _ _ _ r.

Chapter test

1 Which word is misspelt?

a visualise **b** minimise **c** analise **d** improvise

2 Circle the correct verb in this sentence.

Possums and gliders is/are nocturnal.

3 Circle the correct verb is this sentence.

The orchestra is/are tuning its instruments.

4 Which sentence is correctly punctuated? __

a Its' my turn now. **b** Its my turn now. **c** It's my turn now

CHAPTER 10

Factual description

STRUCTURE

title conveys information about text content

***introduction** tells us:*
- *what is happening*
- *who is doing it*
- *where it is being done*

body of description

3 paragraphs:
1. *the spider itself*
2. *milking process*
3. *facts about spider*

conclusion:
- *details of introduction expanded*
- *purpose of milking revealed*

Milking funnel-webs

A window into the spider laboratory at the Australian Reptile Park at Somersby just north of Sydney allows visitors to watch Lyn Abra 'milk' funnel-webs for their precious toxin. Using a glass pipette attached to a suction pump, she agitates an adult spider, sucking up the venom as it emerges from its fangs.

Scanning the rows of captive funnel-webs, Lyn brought a jar down. I peered inside and felt a sudden fight-or-flight adrenalin surge. Sitting impassively in its glass prison was a spider you couldn't ignore—a truly impressive specimen. At around 35 millimetres long, she was about as large as a Sydney funnel-web gets. When Lyn removed the lid I shuffled back a few paces. 'That's one of the biggest fallacies about funnel-webs,' she assured me, 'They don't jump.' She added that the other popular myth about their chasing people is also untrue.

Enthralled, I witnessed the excitable and unpredictable nature for which the funnel-web is renowned. With only the slightest provocation—a pipette touched lightly on her legs—she reared up, front legs raised high, head back, fangs on display. Additional gentle stimulation brought two glistening drops of venom to the ends of her fangs. Then with remarkable speed she snapped down on the pipette with a force normally used to drive her fangs through the hard external skeletons of the small invertebrates that make up the majority of the funnel-web's diet.

Funnel-webs are thought to have a preference for millipedes but they aren't particularly fussy eaters, their diet extending to small lizards. They usually feed at night, waiting just inside their silk-lined burrows, their webs sometimes more like flattened tubes than funnels. Silk trip-lines radiate outwards and anything of a manageable size that sets them vibrating is ambushed.

Lyn's interest in these deadly creatures began, she told me, when she was a child, and was encouraged after she joined the Reptile Park in 1967 and its funnel-web-milking program in the early 1970s. An antivenene was eventually developed in 1980. The reptile park is the sole supplier of the venom used by CSL Ltd. to produce the life-saving pharmaceutical.

(Extract from an article by Karen McGhee in *Australian Geographic*)

LANGUAGE FEATURES

- *must convey all necessary information to allow reader to know the process and the spider*
- *must avoid emotion*
- *must be impartial*

several facts incorporated into each sentence

very few adjectives—only those essential to clarify facts, e.g. the spider's nature and construction of burrow

much information conveyed by verbs

scientific terms and measurements

concise description of ambush (one sentence only)

dates and facts

Comprehension

1 Underline the correct answer. Funnel-webs are milked for venom:

a to limit their ability to kill **b** to supply a pharmaceutical company

2 What is one common myth about funnel-webs? ______________________________

3 What words in the passage suggest the following:

a A funnel-web does not just happen on its food but sets out to trap it. ______________

b A funnel-web usually eats creatures without backbones. ______________________

4 A pipette is a hollow tube. Is this true or false? ______________

5 Underline the correct answer. Funnel-web fangs are so strong because they are:

a weapons **b** tools

6 Underline the correct answer. CSL Ltd:

a houses Lyn's laboratory **b** developed the first antivenene for funnel-web bites

c is the present producer of an anti-venene

7 Underline the correct alternative. Funnel-webs do/do not catch their food by direct attack.

8 Circle the correct answer.

Lyn Abra's interest in funnel-webs began:

a in 1967 **b** in the early 1970s **c** when she was a child **d** in 1980

9 Circle the correct answer.

The sole supplier of funnel-web venom is CSL Ltd. True/False

Writing skills

1 Underline the correct answer. How many facts are presented in the first paragraph?

a three **b** five **c** seven **d** more than eight

2 Underline the correct answer. The few adjectives present in the first paragraph:

a add colour and interest **b** define nouns more precisely

c engage the reader's emotions **d** are intended to frighten the reader

3 Which part of the text introduces the subject of the work done at the Reptile Park's laboratory?

____

4 What evidence does the writer offer to support the statement that funnel-webs are excitable and unpredictable? ______________________________

5 Why does the writer use the adjective *remarkable* in the phrase *remarkable speed*? ______________

____

6 Underline the correct answer. *Remarkable speed* contrasts with an earlier description of the spider *sitting impassively*. The effect of this contrast is to:

a confuse with contradiction **b** underline the unpredictability of the spider

c accentuate the fright of the writer

7 Underline which of the following is nearest in meaning to *glistening*?

a glittering **b** flashing **c** gleaming **d** sparkling

8 How do we know that the funnel-web spider and not Dr Lyn Abra is the main subject of this article? Give two reasons for your answer. ______________________________

____

9 Underline the correct answer. The verb *milk* is in inverted commas because:

a it is a book title **b** it is a quotation

c it is a word borrowed from an apparently unrelated field

10 Underline the correct answer. Factual description primarily:

a conveys information **b** involves the reader emotionally **c** challenges the imagination

Vocabulary

argue	inform	describe	record	outline
define	manageable	antivenene	pharmaceutical	invertebrates

1 The first six words refer to what factual writing can do. Commit them to memory.

2 Break the four big words into syllables. Underline their difficult parts. Then, using the Look, Cover, Write, Check method, learn to spell them.

Focus on punctuation

Apostrophe of possession

An **apostrophe** can indicate ownership. Simply add an apostrophe then an 's' to the end of a singular noun, e.g.
Julia's skateboard, Sam's fishing rod, Benny Elias's joggers

1 Show ownership in the following:

Carly___ horse, Mr Freeth___ car, Edward Lear___ limericks, Don Bradman___ bat

If a singular noun ends in 's' , it is also acceptable to place only an apostrophe at the end of the noun, e.g.
Benny Elias' joggers

2 Show ownership in the following.

Marcus___ watch, Mrs Remedios___ house, Paul Petronas___ fishing fleet

Most plural nouns end in 's'. To show ownership here simply add an apostrophe after the 's', e.g.
the three scientists' discovery.

3 Show ownership in the following.

six officers___ uniforms, all the cows___ horns, some classes___ home-rooms.

If a plural noun does not end in 's' place the apostrophe after its plural part and add 's', e.g.
the mice's tails, all the sheep's wool

4 Show ownership in the following.

the cattle___ show preparation, the fish___ secretive behaviour, the people___ President

5 Add apostrophes where appropriate.

a A barristers assistant is a junior counsel.

b A dog is mans best friend.

c The fleets catch was stolen.

d Peter swapped his ball for Johns, John swapped that for Freds and Mick didn't want anyones ball.

6 Cross (✗) any sentence where the apostrophe is misplaced.

a Mrs Andersons' cat is black. ___

b All six boy's surfboards were freshly waxed. ___

c Marcuss' drum kit is all steel. ___

d Lucas' jeans are ripped across the knees. ___

7 This sentence is correctly punctuated. True/False

We have lovely new potatoes' for sale today.

Select a word

Choose synonyms from the vocabulary list.

1 tell ______________________

2 dispute ______________________

3 specify ______________________

4 depict ______________________

5 docile ______________________

6 spinelesss ______________________

Grammar

Adjectives and adjectival phrases

Adjectives describe nouns. They tell us the colour, shape, size, number and even mood of the noun, e.g.

Five happy yellow chickens cheeped as we lifted the heavy blanket from their circular pen.

1 Underline the adjectives in the following.

a A flight of nineteen wild ducks flew over the lake.

b It was an old boat with faded paint and an old-fashioned rudder.

c Bring the full can here and put the empty one in the recycling bin.

2 Underline the adjectives in these sentences from the text.

a I witnessed the excitable and unpredictable nature for which the funnel-web is renowned.

b Additional gentle stimulation brought two glistening drops of venom to the ends of her fangs.

An **adjectival phrase** is a group of words without a verb that describes a noun, e.g.

The train, the famous 3801, steamed towards Katoomba.

3 Underline the adjectival phrases in the following.

a Lal Patel, the boy at the surf carnival, reached the national finals.

b He had to mind his sister, the three-year-old, while his parents were out.

c *Riverdance* was a popular dance show from Ireland, land of music and poetry.

4 Insert these adjectival phrases in the appropriate sentences below.

i the sleek brushtail possum **ii** a fragile ornament **iii** a flimsy piece of silk

a My shirt, ______________________, was no protection against the cold.

b Theo, ______________________, sat blinking in the torch light.

c The vase, ______________________, fell from the mantelpiece.

5 Insert these adjectives and adjectival phrases in the text that follows.

deep free unpredictable volunteers all of them popular

Surf lifesavers, ________________________, spend their ______ time patrolling _____________ beaches to ensure no one gets swept out by an ______________ rip or slips into ________ water when a sandbar collapses.

Word study

1 Insert an appropriate verb from the vocabulary list.

a Miss Brown will __________________________ the attendance figures for today.

b 'Just _________________________ what happened; I don't need any excuses,' snapped the conductor.

c Please __________________________ Year 7 that Recess will be extended.

d Just __________________________ the main points of your case.

e The Affirmative will now __________________________ that the Olympics has lost the amateur spirit.

f __________________________ the characteristics of an invertebrate.

2 Which verbs from the vocabulary list could be used with these phrases?

a to __________________________ information on disc

b to __________________________ the case for lowering the age to vote

c to __________________________ the exact nature of the new compound

d to __________________________ the flamboyant new rock star in all his glory

3 Complete these sentences with a word from the vocabulary list.

a Antibiotics are manufactured by ____________________ companies.

b A well-trained dog is a _____________________ dog.

c A tiger snake bite must be treated with an ___________________.

d The jellyfish is an example of an ____________________.

Word usage

The toad

On the streets they called him the 'chanchu'—'The Toad'. He was tall for a Chinese, but lightly built. He had a thin face with a mouth so wide that the line of his thin lips seemed to split his face. He also had an ability to squeeze himself through the smallest cracks. He was a thief and he was ruthless. The people of the streets and markets spat out his name with loathing.

The man left the lane-way, vaulting over a low wall into a concrete channel. He started running bent double down this channel, one of the deep drains common in this part of the city. Ahead was a stream of thick grey water pouring from a side pipe. He dared not get himself wet, and he leapt the stream as he ran in bare feet and the slapping sound of his footfalls was covered by the rattle of the wind.

(An extract from *Murder at the City Wall* by Xu Ning, Wyong, NSW, Reid Books, 1998)

1 This is a good example of factual description.

a It contains clearly expressed facts. How many can you find in paragraph 1? ______________________

b It conveys information through dramatic verbs as well as adjectives. Find such a verb in the last sentence of paragraph 1. ______________________

c Underline the correct answer. Its information is logically arranged. In this passage the logical arrangement is based on:

i sequence of ideas **ii** sequence of time **iii** sequence of incidents

d The writing is compact, detailed and precise. We learn about the Toad's height, his features, his skill, his nickname, his occupation and his character all in how many lines? ______________________

2 Find synonyms among the underlined words of the passage for:

a pitiless ______________________ **b** disgust ______________________

c alley-way ______________________ **d** leaping ______________________

3 Using words underlined in the passage compete the following.

a The boy ______________________ from the bike just before it struck the bus.

b A fine ______________________ of superheated air escaped from the pressure valve.

c Flyweight boxing is for ______________________ fighters.

d He ______________________ not make a sound lest his enemy hear him.

Quick think

Factual writing demands accurate terminology. Any old word will not do, e.g. *wind*. Winds are not all the same. They vary in strength, motion and location.

Can you name these winds?

1 a dangerous American wind funnel t ____________ o

2 a wild storm g ____________ e

3 a light wind b ____________ e

4 a very faint wind z ____________ r

5 a sudden rush of wind g ____________ t

6 a circular tropical wind t ____________ n

Proofreading

Insert missing punctuation and capital letters, and correct spelling.

Be careful, paul's father warned him as he set off with his mates to camp in the royal national park. Its january and the funelwebs are about. Paul grined.

They wont bite us, dad were to big to ambush

Don't laugh, son. The funnelwebs bite is fatal if you dont receive antivenene in time.

Idiom

Explain:

1 John's a real stick-in-the-mud. ______________________

____

2 You're in over your head, son. Try something simpler. ______________________

____

Writing paragraphs and whole texts

1 Rearrange the following facts to make a sensible piece of factual writing about starting a fire without matches. You need only rearrange the letters on the line below these facts.

a The shavings carefully packed in the hollow eventually began to smoke.

b The pointed stick twirled quickly between his palms produced friction heat in the hollow.

c His efforts were rewarded first with a fine shower of sparks and then with a quick bright flame.

d In a deep hollow at the end of a large piece of old dry wood he inserted the end of a pointed stick.

e Clancy bent over and blew gently across the shavings while continuing to twirl the stick between his palms.

f Within five minutes this single flame was coaxed into a crackling fire with the addition of dry grasses and small twigs.

____

2 Look around your room. In four lines describe its layout. Do <u>not</u> describe its tidiness or untidiness. Simply explain, as if for a police report, exactly where everything is in relation to everything else in the room.

____

____

____

____

3 Write a brief factual description of one of the following, including details of size, appearance, habitat, diet and lifestyle. Avoid suggestion of any kind of emotion about the creature. The first sentence is written for you—just insert the nouns.

a African elephant **b** Bengal tiger **c** Canadian beaver **d** New Zealand kiwi

The ______ is found only in ________________.

____

____

____

____

____

____

Chapter test

1 Which underlined word is an adjective?

An <u>irritating</u> blowfly buzzed <u>drearily</u> at the window. ______________

2 Write the appropriate adjectival phrase in the space.

an elderly grey pony, a large pink pig

Albert, ________________________, has a small wiggly tail.

3 Which sentence is correctly punctuated? __

a My fathers brother's son is my cousin.

b My fathers' brother's son is my cousin.

c My father's brother's son is my cousin.

d My father's brothers' son is my cousin.

CHAPTER 11

Advertisement

STRUCTURE

headline (introduction)

main statement of sale product

product illustration

LANGUAGE FEATURES

celebrity quotation to underline desirability of product

acknowledgement of quotation source

paragraph of complete sentences

use of second person pronouns ('you') to involve reader personally

repetition for emphasis

point form list of selling points

'A world class program for a world class soccer match' – Mark Bosnich

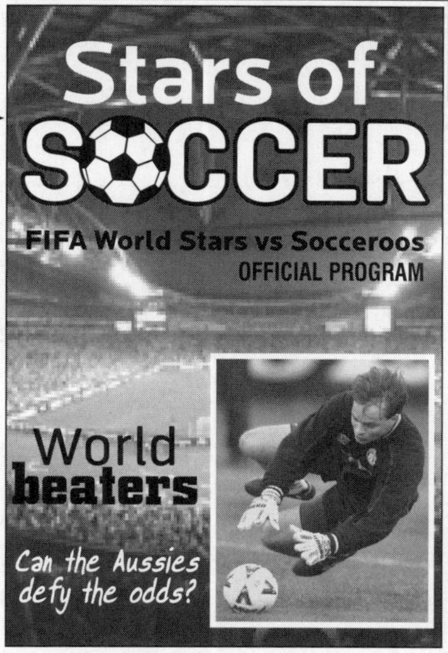

Superstar goalkeeper Mark Bosnich will have to be at his best when the Socceroos take on the FIFA World Stars in Sydney. To be on your toes for the historic clash, get your copy of *Stars of Soccer*, the official program for the official opening of Stadium Australia, the Olympic Stadium.

- Features on Harry Kewell, Mark Viduka, Christian Vieri
- Full player profiles from both teams
- Coaches' tactics
- Best soccer team of all time
- Night's entertainment, including Parade of Champions

Stadium Australia

ON SALE NOW at newsagents or call [03] 9292 1234

selling points

details of availability

bold print facts-only statement

Comprehension

1 Underline the correct answer. This advertisement is selling:

a soccer match tickets **b** soccer match programs

2 Underline the correct answer. The program is for:

a the official opening of Stadium Australia **b** the FIFA World Stars Series

3 What position does Bosnich play? ____________________

4 In what part of the day will the opening match be played? ____________________

5 Why was the stadium built? ____________________

6 How can you buy a ticket to this match? ____________________

7 Australia is favoured to win the World Stars Series. Is this true or false? ____________________

8 Quote the line from the advertisement that justifies your last answer. ______________________

____

9 What are the two essential points of this advertisement? ______________________

Writing skills

1 Underline the correct answer. The heading is in bold print:

a to use up white space **b** to catch the reader's eye

c because it is the most important fact in the advertisement

2 Why has the writer used a quotation from Mark Bosnich to head the advertisement? ______________

____

3 Underline the correct answer. A *feature* is:

a a mention **b** a byline **c** an article **d** an extended written or photographic study

4 What repeated word underlines the international character of the Series? ______________

5 This advertisement originally appeared in colour. Colour printing is expensive. Why did the advertisers go to the extra expense of colour in this advertisement? ______________

6 The advertiser has used colloquial language. Write down two examples from the main paragraph.

____

____

7 Underline two correct answers. Colloquial language is used because it is:

a the language of the targeted reader **b** the language of the advertising agency

c a way of establishing emotional contact with the reader **d** a space-saving device

8 Underline which of these are not valid reasons. Formal language would not have been appropriate in this advertisement because:

a it lacks excitement **b** it has limited reading appeal **c** the advertiser lacked the necessary skills

d it does not have immediate reader identification **e** advertising space is costly

f soccer fans are not good readers

9 The advertisement highlights five phrases with black dots. Why? ______________

10. Insert the missing letters. The top and bottom of the advertisement are both printed in bold. This is an example of b _ l _ _ ce in text layout.

11 Underline the most accurate answer. Using this advertisement as an example, the purpose of advertising is:

a to promote **b** to sell **c** to persuade **d** to inform

Vocabulary

legendary	**famous**	**admirable**	**renowned**	**celebrated**
notorious	**despicable**	**abominable**	**ruthless**	**decadent**

1 Learn these character adjectives in two groups: 'Good' and 'Bad'.

2 Underline any vowel easily missed, e.g. 'a' in *legendary* and 'i' in *abominable*. Then use the Look, Cover, Write, Check method to learn the words in the list.

Focus on punctuation

Apostrophe of possession

Remember:

- Plural nouns in possession of something are followed by an apostrophe, e.g. *all the puppies' bowls, two kittens' whiskers*
- If a plural noun is collective it adds 's, e.g. *the crew's galley, the flock's shepherd*

1 Add apostrophes of possession to the plural nouns underlined.

a Several students books were burned in the fire. **b** All dogs collars should carry identity discs.

c Both parents jobs were made redundant. **d** That books cover is torn.

2 Add two apostrophes of possession in each sentence.

a Martina inherited both her sisters clothes but Evas fitted her best.

b Ming Lees fathers business is doing better than many of their friends businesses.

c Little Pauls illness was so contagious it soon became everyones.

d The lions roar as they went hunting set every creatures teeth on edge.

e Most nocturnal animals eyes are round like the barn owls eyes.

3 Put in any missing apostrophes.

a Peter borrowed his brother Johns compass and two friends camping gear.

b He confiscated all the spies infra-red goggles.

c A buffalo herds hooves could be heard thundering across the plain.

d The prides cubs slept in the sun beside their lioness mothers.

Select a word

By changing or deleting the final syllable or adding an extra suffix, write these adjectives as nouns, e.g. *legendary—legend*

1 famous ____________________ **2** admirable ____________________

3 notorious ____________________ **4** renowned ____________________

5 decadent ____________________ **6** ruthless ____________________

Grammar

Adjectives: comparative & superlative degree forms

Adjectives are not all the same. They say the same kind of thing but in different degrees.

Simple adjectives are factual. **Comparative adjectives** compare one thing with another. **Superlative adjectives** are the strongest form of the adjective.

The different forms are made by adding *~er* or *~est* to the simple adjective, e.g. *big* (simple), *bigger* (comparative), *biggest* (superlative)

1 Complete this table. The first is done for you.

Simple	Comparative	Superlative
pretty	prettier	prettiest
ugly		ugliest
large		largest
	taller	
long		

Some adjectives change degree with the addition of *more* or *most* instead of changing themselves, e.g. *humorous* (simple), *more humorous* (comparative), *most humorous* (superlative)

These adjectives, when expressing a lesser degree, use *less* or *least* in place of *more* and *most*, e.g. *serious* (simple), *less serious* (comparative), *least serious* (superlative)

2 Complete this table using *more* and *most*.

Simple	Comparative	Superlative
sensible	more sensible	most sensible
	more dependable	
		most reliable
trustworthy		
	more malicious	
		most honest

3 Complete this table using *less* and *least*.

Simple	Comparative	Superlative
nervous		least nervous
famous	less famous	
	less careful	least careful
anxious		
dangerous		least dangerous

4 Complete using the correct form of the adjective.

a Mr Nguyen is __________ (old) than Mr Sung.

b Dolores is the __________ (young) of the two Ruiz sisters.

c Anthony was the ______________ (frightened) of the boys and ran from the scene.

d The lyrics of this song are silly but the lyrics of that one are even __________ (silly).

e Rachel, the school's fastest sprinter, was the ____________ (worried) race competitor.

Word study

1 Using words from the vocabulary list complete the following.

a Hercules was a ______________________ hero.

b Jack the Ripper was a ______________________ London murderer.

c The Red Cross is ______________________ for its work in war-torn lands.

d Phar Lap was a______________________ Australian race horse.

2 By substituting one word from the vocabulary list reverse the meaning of each of the following. (You may need to change the indefinite articles, *a* and *an*, too.)

a He was a truly admirable individual. ______________________

b The queen ruled in a merciful and generous manner. ______________________

c The old man had lived an upright life. ______________________

d Seeping gases from the swamp smelt fragrant. ______________________

3 Circle the appropriate adjectives in these sentences.

a Ned Kelly was a famous/notorious bushranger.

b Bullying is admirable/despicable behaviour.

c St George is the legendary/renowned slayer of dragons.

4 Write the appropriate list adjective for each.

a a soup made of gravel, weed and earth and flavoured with snail oil ______________________

b someone who doesn't care who is hurt as long as he wins ______________________

c an eating, drinking, lazing, waited-on, non-working lifestyle ______________________

Word usage

A: Cheap, cheap, cheap!

Looking for an investment or first home? Then don't miss out on this one. Sitting on a large block, the home offers 2 bedrooms and is loaded with potential. With a little elbow grease and imagination this home will be transformed into a lovely cottage. Homes in this price range don't last long, so don't delay in asking us for more information or come along and inspect this Saturday. Price: $150 000.

B: Nursed back to life!

This double brick home has been nursed back to life and offers the best of both worlds with a successful combination of period style and modern comfort. Ornate ceilings, picture and china rails, open fire place, polished floors, leadlight windows, bay window, window seats and sweeping verandah take you a step back in time. A new timber kitchen of red cedar, 2 bathrooms, 3 bedrooms plus study, entertaining area and garage will bring you back to the comforts of modern living. This home must be inspected to be appreciated. Price: $750 000.

1 **a** Compare the two headings of texts A and B and then insert the missing letters. They say one house has been r _ _ _ v _ t _ d and the other one has been n _ _ l _ c t _ d.

b Match the underlined words and phrases in the house advertisements with the meanings below.

i highly decorated ________________

ii long and wide ________________

iii can be improved ________________

iv work ________________

v window jutting out from main wall ________________

vi belonging to a particular time in history ________________

2 Some real estate advertising language has its own meaning for words. This kind of language is called jargon. For example, *a handyman's special* is jargon for a rundown property in need of a lot of repair. Prospective buyers have to read very carefully.

Answer True (T) or False (F) to the following.

a If you bought a *renovator's delight* you'd have nothing to do. ________________

b If your new house was *compact* you could accommodate three people. ________________

c If your house *just needs a little TLC* it is in perfect condition. ________________

Quick think

1 Advertisements often contain abbreviations and **acronyms** (initials linked together as a word). What do the following mean?

a TLC ________________ **b** ASAP ________________

c ONO ________________ **d** AH ________________

2 Different items for sale have their own advertising jargon. What would you be buying if an advertisement included these terms?

a All round sound plus mags and alloys ________________

b Ensuite and walk-in robe ________________

c X breed, small, papers, microchip, wormed, vacc. ________________

3 Conditions of sale also include jargon.

a If you bought a car on an *as is, where is* basis, underline which of the following would be the most likely scenario.

i You would find it in perfect condition. **ii** The vendor (seller) would deliver to you.

iii You would have to tow it home.

b If you bought a house on a *WI/WO* (walk in/walk out) basis, would you expect or not expect to experience delays before moving in? ________________

Proofreading

Make all necessary spelling and punctuation corrections in the following passage.

Soccers my favorite sport and I want to play with the socceroos when Im older. My ambishun is to mach peles record. his fame is allmost legendery among soccar players.

Idiom

Explain:

1 Come on, use a bit of elbow grease to get the job done properly. ____________________

____

2 You can't sit on the fence in this discussion of wind power versus solar power. ____________________

____

Writing paragraphs and whole texts

1 Rearrange the phrases in Box A to create an advertisement for a car sale in Box B. Read the phrases carefully and arrange them according to the importance they would have as information for a potential buyer.

A	B
a Heaps of bargains	
b Stocktake sale	
c Be quick	
d Morry's Motors	
e 433 Parramatta Road	
f Drive away today	
g Auburn	
h Finance available	
i All makes and models	

2 You have bought a new skateboard and wish to sell your old one. Write an advertisement to place in the local paper. Its details are as follows: two years old, some chips and scratches, good brand name, rollers slightly worn, one owner since new, no accidents. (Note: include your own details so a buyer can contact you.)

____

____

____

____

____

____

3 1976 holden sedan, unreg., some body rust, motor OK, as is, where is, $1000 ono. Ph. 02 6222 3333 ah only.

Write a paragraph explaining why you would or would not buy the car in this advertisement.

____

____

____

____

____

____

4 You are introducing a new line of teenage clothing under the brand name FLAME. Write an advertisement for FLAME sportswear for teenagers to fit the front page of a tri-fold catalogue. Check that you include all relevant information including where it can be bought. Use a variety of print sizes and styles, graphics (e.g. sketches, diagrams) and, most importantly, market-appropriate language (language your buyers use).

____

____

____

____

____

____

____

____

____

____

Chapter test

1 Write the correct form of the adjective in the space.

This option is ____________ than that one.

a bad **b** more bad **c** baddest **d** worse

2 Correct the adjective in this sentence.

This is the <u>crankier</u> cat I have ever met. _________

3 Write the correct form of the adjective *placid* in the space.

We were all calm but she was __________________ of us all.

4 Which sentence is correctly punctuated?

a Mr Grants' wife advertised: Ripe tomatoes' just a dollar a kilo!

b Mr Grant's wife advertised: Ripe tomatoes just a dollar a kilo!

c Mr Grants' wife advertised: Ripe tomatoe's just a dollar a kilo!

d Mr Grant's wife advertised: Ripe tomatoes's just a dollar a kilo!

CHAPTER 12

Sports article

STRUCTURE

headline: makes main point of article—gridiron is stop-start

***introduction**: tells what article is about—game and venue*

***body of article**: paragraphs each make one point, e.g.*
- *big players*
- *slow play*
- *examples of stop-play*
- *spectator response*

***conclusion**: emphasises main point—it's slow all the time*

When going gets tough, tough take a break

America rejected our lamb and sent us their beef. Stamped US prime, it was on display at Stadium Australia yesterday as the San Diego Chargers and the Denver Broncos played the American Bowl.

The venue is not far from where cattle of similar weight to the players compete for best-in-breed at the Easter Show.

Giant young men with the same DNA as small apartment buildings crashing into each other with confusing gusto transports Americans to sporting enchantment.

It tends to leave Australians, used to greater fluency and continuity in their football codes, less enthused.

These players take more breaks than wharfies used to have in their old contracts.

They stop for television commercial breaks, they stop to run on and off the field, they stop for up to half-a-dozen time-outs, they stop when there is a kick to be taken, they stop after a pass is caught, they stop to hear umpires explain penalties and they stop to measure distances.

It's amazing that a country like America, whose economy and social structure are based upon being quicker and slicker, can enthuse about taking three hours to play one hour of football.

There was at least a special cheer for Chargers punter and former AFL player Darren Bennett.

'I was very nervous,' he said.

'But the cheering was a wonderful adrenalin rush for me.'

It was, if nothing else, a valiant attempt to showcase the game before an inquiring audience with mixed results.

Former Australian cricket captain Ian Chappell was seen leaving the Stadium at half-time. Maybe he came back.

2UE commentator Mike Carlton lasted the full game and was succinct as he left.

'I've had more fun,' he said.

A quick poll in the stands revealed a tight core of gridiron supporters coupled with others just having a day out.

'I was disappointed,' said one man. 'It never seems to get started.'

Another said, 'It's too stop-start.'

And so it went on.

(Excerpt from an article by Ray Chesterton in the *Daily Telegraph*)

LANGUAGE FEATURES

play on words

very short paragraphs typical of newspapers

colourful comparisons

multiple repetition and multiple examples

limiting phrases, suggesting that there was nothing else much to praise

quotations

Comprehension

1 Underline the correct answer. This article is about

a baseball **b** American football **c** Australian football

2 Darren Bennett played in this game. Is this true or false? ____________________

3 Underline the correct answer. Crowd reaction could be described as:

a muted **b** enthusiastic **c** supportive **d** unenthusiastic

4 Fill in the blanks.
Gridiron lacks the ____________________ and the ____________________ of Australian football.

5 What was the main complaint about the nature of gridiron? ____________________

6 Do you think Chesterton agrees with Carlton's view of the game? Give a reason for your answer.

____

7 Darren Bennett's 'adrenalin rush' refers to a sense of:

a contentment **b** new energy **c** excitement **d** competitiveness

Writing skills

1 This headline plays with words. What is the popular saying that it plays with?

____

2 Underline the correct answers. The <u>effect</u> of this headline's word play is to:

a sum up what's wrong with gridiron **b** make fun of the Americans

c establish a light tone for the article rather than a serious one

3 What words in the headline sum up what the writer thought was wrong with gridiron?

____

4 The first sentence plays with *lamb* and *beef*. The *lamb* refers to American restrictions on imports of Australian lamb at that time. To what does the *beef* refer? ____________________

5 Underline the correct answer. The purpose of the beef image is to emphasis the:

a muscle of the players **b** bulk of the players **c** slowness of the players

6 The word *giant* is reinforced by a comparison to emphasise size. What is the comparison?

____

7 Fill in the missing letters. Words such as *premiership* and *time-out* are examples of sporting j _ _ _ _ _ .

8 Underline the correct answer. The use of words like these gives:

a information **b** colour **c** authenticity to the article

9 Does Chesterton use the writing technique of repetition or short sentences to demonstrate how often the flow of the game is broken? ____________________

10 Underline the correct answer. The purpose of quoting Mike Carlton and referring to Ian Chappell is to:

a demonstrate that Chesterton knows famous people

b lend authority to his own view of gridiron

c double as a social commentator as well as a sports commentator

11 Underline the correct alternative. The tone of this article is light and flippant/critical and serious.

12 Underline the correct answer. The purpose of this article is to:

a report impartially **b** report critically **c** report negatively **d** report dismissively

Vocabulary

humorous	jocular	jovial	genial	benign
sarcastic	acerbic	satirical	malicious	biased

Look carefully at these words. Underline the silent 'g', the 'c' used for 's' sounds and the 'g' used for the 'j' sound. Underline the *~or* in *humorous*. Say the words containing these out loud as you look at them. Then use the Look, Cover, Write, Check method to learn the words. You may need to repeat this process several times.

Focus on punctuation

Hyphens and dashes

- **Hyphens** are used to break a word at a convenient syllable so it can be completed on the next line, e.g.

  The tragic earthquake that shook Turkey in 1999 was succeeded by seismo-
  logical activity in Greece and Taiwan.

- Hyphens also join two or more words that are linked together to form an adjective, e.g.

  He was a hamburger-munching, stubby-in-hand armchair sportsman.

1 Hyphenate these words at a convenient syllable.

instruction ____________ production ____________ absolutely ____________

2 Insert hyphens to create two-word adjectives in the following.

a Australians sometimes think of Americans as baggy trousered, cap wearing baseball fanatics.

b Americans probably consider Australians as sausage sizzling, Vegemite loving cricket fanatics.

Dashes separate an aside or short explanation from an initial statement, e.g.

It's very new—I only bought it this morning.

3 Insert dashes where appropriate.

a Rihanna, Katy Perry and Kesha they're the female voices of this decade.

b 'Modern music can't hear a word they're singing,' muttered the old man.

c Whatever's out there and I can't hear it now is obviously stalking us.

4 The hyphenated words are incorrect. Choose the words that should be hyphenated, then write them in the spaces with their hyphens correctly placed.

a Checkshirted rodeo clowns in hats and leather-chaps protect fallen riders. ____________

b He waited for moon-rise before tracking the transmitter fitted wallaby. ____________

c Carla is a multi award winning pianist and con-ductor. ____________

d He loves heavily chromed twin-exhaust, mag wheeled sports cars. ____________

Select a word

Using the suffix ~*ar* write adjectives for these nouns.

1 molecule ____________ **2** cell ____________

3 South Pole ____________ **4** consul ____________

5 angle ____________ **6** nucleus ____________

Grammar

Personal pronouns

Pronouns take the place of nouns. **Personal pronouns** take the place of nouns referring to people. They include such words as *him* and *her*, e.g.
Elise told her parents she was going skating with their neighbours.

1 Underline the personal pronouns.

a His uncle told them to surf between the flags. **b** The band lost all its equipment in the accident.

c 'Your guitar is not here,' his friend told Danny. **d** Our cricket pitch was washed out.

e Their game attracted thousands of spectators.

f Although I am a tall basketball player, he is much taller.

2 Rewrite the following, replacing nouns with personal pronouns wherever possible.

a Kristin invited John and all John's friends over for a video veg-out night. ____________

b Mr Gupta has lost a valuable watch and the watch's case. ____________

c The reporter thought the Americans stopped play too often. ____________

d The boys watched Max shoot six goals in a row. ____________

e Paula found the family's lost dog without the dog's identity tag. ____________

3 Circle the correct personal pronoun.

a All the boys lost all his/their football gear.

b The score board lost all their/its numbers in the high wind.

c We won all your/our matches this season.

d Kirsty believes her skills grow out of the daily practice he/she puts in.

e Competitors must complete our/their/your warm-up sessions before racing.

Word study

1 Insert an appropriate positive adjective from the top row of the vocabulary list.

a The atmosphere around the barbecue was ____________ as the men swapped tales of big fish and customised cars.

b His mother's ________________ expression faded as he confessed to crashing into her daffodil bed on his bike.

c To be truly ________________ a joke must be told in the language style of the listeners.

2 Insert an appropriate negative adjective from the bottom row of the vocabulary list.

a ________________ rumours can destroy someone's reputation overnight.

b 'Studying hard, are we?' was the ________________ comment of Tim's brother when he was watching *Monkey Magic*.

c 'And you'd believe all that?' was the ________________ response of her mother to Sarah's account of George's adventures.

3 Choose an appropriate word from the list to describe these:

a A team leader who only picks tall players ________________

b Santa Claus in a red suit laughing and calling 'Ho, ho, ho' ________________

c Someone who damages other people's things for fun ________________

d Someone speaking briefly and sharply ________________

4 The prefix *mal~* means 'bad'. Complete these negative words.

a	a criminal	mal _f _ _t _ r
b	poorly fed	mal n _ _ r _ _ _ ed
c	an illness	mal _ dy
d	smelling bad	mal _ d _ r _ _ s
e	intending evil	mal _ _ _ lent
f	a defect in shape	malf _ _ m _ tion
g	a curse	mal _ d _ _ tion
h	incorrect performance of work	malp _ _ _ tice

Word usage

Jargon is the word for the special language of groups doing the same thing, e.g. tradespeople, doctors, horse trainers, musicians etc. Like all specialists in their field, sportspeople have their own jargon.

1 Underline any jargon in the following sentence from a sports article.

Delaney, the Australian and Adelaide Thunderbirds' goal attack, led the defending champions against the Adelaide Ravens, shooting 38 goals from 45 attempts.

2 Rewrite the following statement without using the jargon term *drew*.

The Thunderbirds drew with the Ravens.

____

3 Insert the jargon below in the following.

i par **ii** corner **iii** line-out **iv** foil **v** heptathlon

a A fencer must keep the point of her ________________ covered at all times.

b A ________________ will cause delay of play in Rugby Union.

c When the opposing team is awarded a ________________ a soccer goal keeper must be on guard.

d Two over ________________ is an excellent score for a first game of golf.

e Hurdling is included as one of the seven events in a ________________.

4 Words associated with war are often associated with sports writing. Underline the war jargon in the following.

a The defending champion won his third successive victory.

b By the half-time siren there had been little attacking play by the local side.

c When the Fifth Test opened battle lines were drawn—Australia had to win this match or lose the Series to Sri Lanka, who, cock-a-hoop over two wins already, were more than prepared for the fray.

5 Circle the occupations or areas of knowledge to which these examples of jargon belong.

a high voltage:	**i** fishing	**ii** electrical trades	**iii** heavy metal construction
b cumulus:	**i** pillow-making	**ii** banking	**iii** weather reporting
c carat:	**i** goldsmithing	**ii** woodwork	**iii** vegetable-growing
d tonsillectomy:	**i** dentistry	**ii** radiography	**iii** surgery
e tremor:	**i** psychiatry	**ii** seismology	**iii** storm-chasing

Quick think

Match the name to the activity.

a archery **b** fencing **c** polo **d** slalom **e** abseiling

1 _____ team game played on horseback

2 _____ competitive individual activity using bow and arrows

3 _____ two-person activity involving swordplay

4 _____ a zigzag downhill ski race with obstacles

5 _____ individual rope-assisted cliff descent

Proofreading

Carefully proof the following sports report for inclusion in your school magazine. Insert all missing punctuation and correct all misspelt words in the passage. (Hint: a hyphen has been omitted.)

Last wednesday's game agaist duck Creek saw our boys mantain their wining streak. Behind at half time they came back to score three trys and clear too gaols to even the score with five minutes still to go. A great run down the field from smithy saw the ball passed to Johnno, across to Daley and straight into the arms of the man with the fastst feet in hays Park, Charlie Singh. Charlies try was converted by Papadopoulos and once again Hays park had come out on top.

Idiom

Explain:

1 The Kookaburras scored back-to-back wins against the Koels and the Rosellas this season. __________

____

2 That's a line-ball decision I wouldn't like to make. __________

____

Writing paragraphs and whole texts

1 The following sentence is the first sentence of a paragraph about a game lost by a basketball team called the Arrows. The writer is an Arrows supporter.
Although the Arrows lost their match against the Springfeld Warriors, they lost with honour.

Answer each part of this question on the lines following to complete the Arrows supporter's paragraph.

a Which of sentences, X or Y, would be the best one to follow it? ________________

X *The Warriors played hard and we realised early on that the Arrows would not win this match.*

Y *Despite the Warriors' height advantage our team played hard and cleverly.*

b Underline the correct answer. What should come next?
i an example of clever play **ii** an example of the Warriors' goal scoring ability

c Write a sentence that does what your answer to **b** suggests, as the third sentence of this report.

d Invent two players' names and write the fourth sentence about those two players, ending the sentence with … *a winning partnership in the fourth quarter.*

e Your fifth sentence will begin:
Other players who excelled on the court were …

f Sentence 6 will tell us what those players did that was excellent. (You might refer to defence tactics, attacking skills, ball-passing techniques, speed on court.)

g Conclude your paragraph with a sentence that ends with the words:
… *it was an honourable defeat and no cause for despair so early in the season.*

____

____

____

____

____

____

____

____

____

____

____

2 Remembering that newspaper writing is characterised by short paragraphs and that a paragraph deals with one idea only, break up the following passage into paragraphs (by inserting [) so that it is suitable for printing as a sports report in a newspaper.

The Walmer Ringers will attempt their third straight premiership this Saturday against the other dominant regional club, Newgrange. The game will kick off at 3 pm at South Oval and a big crowd of local support is expected to counter the bussed-in support from Newgrange. Walmer has been the dominant team of the last decade, winning premierships in first grade in 2007, 2009 and 2010. First grade were also runners up in 2006 and 2008. 'This will be four grand final appearances in a row for some members of this team,' said Les Gregg, Ringers President. 'And they know what has to be done to win.'

3 Write one sentence for each of five of the following sports in which you describe something happening using the jargon of that sport.

Any code of Football, Hockey, Cricket, Baseball, Basketball, Soccer, Netball, Surfing, Skiing, Scuba Diving, Abseiling, Canoeing, Rowing

a ____

____

b ____

____

c ____

____

d ____

____

e ____

____

Chapter test

1 Circle the correct personal pronoun.

This tennis racquet has lost most of his/its strings.

2 Which sentence contains the correct personal pronoun? Circle the right answer.

a Every girl lost their shoes in the swamp.

b Every girl lost her shoes in the swamp.

3 Circle the correctly hyphenated word.

a swallow-tailed **b** navigati-on **c** residen-tial

4 Circle the sentence containing a misspelling.

a A sarcastic person can offend people.

b Everyone likes a genial person.

c Mrs Carlyle's stories are always humourous.

CHAPTER 13

Song lyric

STRUCTURE

title: suggests theme (idea) of song

verses: each verse is about a different part of the theme (verse 1: don't tell us what to do verse 2: it is our future, not yours)

chorus: sums up the main idea of the song; repeated between verses, the chorus underlines the meaning of the verse

Prisoner of Society

Well we don't need no-one to tell us what to do
Oh yes we're on our own and there's nothing you can do
So we don't need no-one like you to tell us what to do

We don't refer to the past when showing what we've done
The generation gap means the war is never won
The past is in your head
The future's in our hands

'Cos I'm a brat, and I know everything
And I talk back, 'cos I'm not listening
To anything you say
And if you count to three—one, two, three
You'll see it's no emergency
You'll see I'm not the enemy
Just a prisoner of society

Lyrics by Rae Harvey

LANGUAGE FEATURES

colloquial language of target audience (young people who will buy the CD)

repetition of key phrases; regular rhythm (beat—tap out the syllables and listen)

use of first and second person pronouns ('I', 'us' and 'you') includes listener with singer in song

use of rhyme (see also verses 1 and 2)

Comprehension

1 Underline the correct answer. The voice in this song is that of:

a an unemployed person **b** a rebel **c** a teenager **d** a convict

2 Underline the correct answer. The main point of his/her complaint is:

a adults talk about the past **b** the generation gap
c adults tell young people what to do **d** adults talk about emergencies

3 By implication who does refer to the past when *showing what we've done*? ______

4 What war will never be won and why? ______

______

5 Underline the correct answer. For the speaker talking back is an act of:

a defiance **b** obstruction **c** silliness **d** rudeness

6 Whose words is the speaker quoting in the chorus? ______

7 The chorus could be described as a plea for understanding. Do you agree? Give a reason for your answer. ______

______

Writing skills

1 Underline the correct answer. The language of this song could be described as:

a complex **b** colloquial **c** stilted **d** formal

2 The tone of these lyrics could be described by three of the following adjectives. Underline the incorrect one.

a provocative **b** challenging **c** forceful **d** insincere

3 In what line is the idea of defiance introduced? ______________________________

4 Underline the correct answer. *We're on our own* tells us how youth see themselves. The words suggest:

a independence **b** rebellion **c** revolution **d** peer togetherness

5 What words tell us that youth is objecting to adults saying, 'When I was young …'?

____

6 Underline the correct answer. The phrase *generation gap* is:

a a clever phrase **b** a cliché **c** an example of rhyme

7 The chorus contains two ideas. What are they? ______________________________

8 Underline the correct answer. When the singer says, *I'm a brat* etc, this is an example of:

a exaggeration **b** irony **c** an antonym

9 The instruction *count to three* is usually preceded by 'Take a deep breath'. Why has the writer included counting to three in the lyrics? ______________________________

10 This song is called 'Prisoner of Society'. Why is it a more appropriate title than 'I'm a Brat'?

____

Vocabulary

ballad	**harmony**	**melody**	**lyric**	**arrangement**
synchronise	**enemy**	**generation**	**emergency**	**society**

The first six words are musical terms commonly used in writing about musicians and their music. You should memorise them for use when you write about your favourite group or CD.

Many words end in *~ise* (e.g. *synchronise*). You will sometimes see them spelt *~ize*. This is incorrect.

The last four words occur in 'Prisoner of Society'. Underline these words where they occur, study their meaning in context and then learn to spell them using the Look, Cover, Write, Check method. Pay special attention to the word *enemy*.

Focus on punctuation

Colons (:)

Colons can:

- separate a speaker from his or her lines in a script, e.g.
  Mickey: I want to come too.
- separate a major fact from all its component parts, e.g.
  Details you requested:
  I am 14. I attend Ibrox Park High School. I am in Year 7.
- introduce a list, e.g.
  green vegetables: spinach, broccoli, bok choi, silver beet, cabbage and choy sum

Insert colons and commas as required.

1 As per your order one set of guitar strings two plectrums and three intermediate level score sheets.

2 List the band members by instrument trumpeters saxophonists clarinet players a flautist and a bassoonist.

3 Priest Do you have any last words to say, Ned?

Ned Kelly Such is life.

4 The order of procession into the hall will be as follows Year 7 Year 8 and Year 10 in that order.

5 Here's the list of camping equipment needed a two-man tent a tomahawk a frying pan and saucepan a box of matches and a can of insect spray.

6 Don't feed the wildlife no biscuits lollies cakes fruit meats or any other foods.

7 His last instructions proceeds of the estate to be passed to the Foundation for Lost Dogs.

8 Interviewer Why did you take up playing the bassoon?

Select a word

Find synonyms for these words from the vocabulary list.

1 community ____________________

2 foe ____________________

3 agreement ____________________

4 tune ____________________

5 organisation ____________________

6 serenity ____________________

Grammar

Relative pronouns

Relative pronouns take the place of nouns. They include such words as *who, whom, whose, which, that*, e.g.

Yagan was an Aboriginal warrior <u>who</u> fought against European settlement in West Australia.
Rel. pronoun

1 Underline the relative pronouns.

a To whom did you lend my CD?

b I borrowed the skateboard that you left in the gym.

c Peter, whose parents are overseas, is staying with us.

d Drums, which damage easily, must be handled carefully.

2 Join these sentences using a relative pronoun.

a Kristen has moved to another school. Kristen is my friend.

____

b I delivered a pizza to Mr Jones. Mr Jones is my old neighbour.

____

c We hired a strobe light for the disco. The strobe light was brilliant.

____

d Michael went looking for the dog. The dog had slipped its chain and escaped.

____

3 Write an appropriate relative pronoun in each space.

a The boy __________ won the wind section of the eisteddfod was applauded.

b Mr Saleh, __________ skills as a musician are legendary, is on tour.

c Guitar strings __________ are slack do not produce a good sound.

d Good acoustics, __________ are essential to good music, are rarely found in music venues.

Word study

1 Match these meanings to words from the vocabulary list.

a a story put to music and sung ____________________

b words of a song ____________________

c a piece of music arranged for several instruments or voices ____________________

d a pleasant agreement of sound ____________________

e a musical tune ____________________

2 One word in the vocabuary list means 'to make happen together'. Insert it to compete these sentences.

a '____________________ your watches,' said the tour guide.

b '____________________ audio and visual recordings,' ordered the director.

3 Change these nouns to adjectives by using **suffixes** (syllables added to the ends of words to influence or change their meaning, e.g. *~able, ~ful, ~ious, ~al*).

a melody ____________________ **b** harmony ____________________

c lyric ____________________ **d** society ____________________

4 Change these nouns to verbs by using or deleting suffixes.

a harmony ____________________ **b** arrangement ____________________

c generation ____________________ **d** emergency ____________________

5 Match words from the list to these situations.

a a child bitten by a snake ____________________

b time span between the ages of an uncle and his nephew ____________________

c a careful placing of flowers in a vase ____________________

d three people happily working together ____________________

Word usage

Words often have several meanings. Exact meaning can be understood only in **context**, i.e. where it occurs. Read the following passage carefully.

Reggae

Reggae music is bound up with the history and **a** ____________________ of Jamaica. Its most famous exponent was the late Bob Marley, a slight man whose significance in late twentieth century music is out of all proportion to his size. With his band, The Wailers, Marley brought the **b** ____________________ of the Jamaican people for justice and a decent standard of living to the rest of the world.

Reggae lyrics are written in the vernacular of the streets and the gangs. They speak of the hard life faced by the young who had no **c** ____________________ of doing anything other than cane-cutting for **d** ______________ pay once they left school. Streetwise lyrics appealed to the **e** ______________ youth of Jamaica's back streets but struck a chord with youth in England, America and South Africa as well.

From such impoverished beginnings reggae music has become an international **f** ______________ that spawned rap, even while maintaining its own grasp on the hearts and mind of young people **g** ______________ for change.

1 Fill in the blanks from the list below so that the passage makes sense.

i disenchanted **ii** phenomenon **iii** meagre **iv** impatient
v culture **vi** struggle **vii** prospect

2 Using the same words as you inserted in 'Reggae', complete the sentences below.

a The queue grew ______________ as the hours passed and the ticket office remained closed.

b Refugees clutching their ______________ possessions crossed the border.

c Aboriginal ______________ is valued and protected by the Aboriginal community.

d The ______________ of an eclipse of the sun always worries the superstitious.

e Australian conservationists are ______________ with the rate of progress on lowering greenhouse gas emissions.

3 Insert the most appropriate of the following words to complete the sentences below. You will not need all words listed and you must not repeat a word.

thumped, blared, audition, signal, tune, concert, discordant, insistent,
fanfare, attraction, conducting, challenging, barracks, awful

a The ______________ was conducted in the smaller ______________ hall.

b Drums ______________ and trumpets ______________ as a ______________ to welcome the Queen.

c Your guitar sounds out of ______________ and ______________.

d ______________ massed high school choirs at the Sydney Entertainment Centre is a ______________ task.

e The ______________ beat of dance party music is its main ______________.

Quick think

An **onomatopoeic** word sounds like the sound it refers to, e.g. *meow, hiss, splash.*

1 Match these onomatopoeic verbs to their instruments.

clash, trill, boom, tinkle

a bass drum ______________ **b** xylophone ______________

c piccolo ______________ **d** cymbals ______________

2 There are special verbs that refer to the way some instruments are played.

Underline the correct alternative in each of the following.

a Peter was strumming/plucking his guitar. **b** Penny was blowing/playing her bagpipes .

c Patrick plucked/played the strings of his harp. **d** Phan blew/played his trumpet.

3 Match these tools to their instruments.

plectrum, bow, reed, pedal

a violin ______________________ **b** clarinet ______________________

c guitar ______________________ **d** piano ______________________

Proofreading

Insert missing punctuation, correct misspelt words and insert ([ ) to indicate where a new paragraph should start in the following passage.

> unless your music is what the public wants to here your'e skill will take you nowhere. Aspiring stars must be prepered to play gigs in places they do not like and for money they considder porltry However, there is always the chanc that one day a recordng studeo agent will hear your music in some seady hall and offer a contract exposure promoshen and stardom. When that hapens you'll start a rolercoaster ride that will either make you a celbrity or a one hit wunder who'll be back struming in those dingey halls inside too years.

Idiom

Explain:

1 She was a fish out of water at the Beethoven festival. ______________________

____

2 His song 'Burn' was just a flash in the pan with nothing since. ______________________

____

Writing paragraphs and whole texts

1 Invent three song titles to catch the imagination of a teenage audience. ______________________

____

2 Songwriters sometimes write to be funny. Often they do so in rhyme. Fill in the missing words in these lines from the song 'Bundaberg Rum' written by WN Scott, making sure you read aloud to catch the rhyme and beat (rhythm). Select words from the following list:

spirit, whisky, rum, hair, pimples, acne, stomach, inside, outside

Bundaberg rum, and it's overproof ______________________,

Will tan your ______________________ and grow ______________________ on your bum.

3 Songwriters write about what they see, hear, think and feel. This is a verse of what John Williamson wrote and sings about Mt Isa in Queensland.

> Big galvanised roofs and monster pipes black
> Pink and white clouds from a chimney stack
> Red dust and hawks in the wind out back
> And here I am at the Isa.

Following Williamson's pattern, write a four-line lyric about a place you know (perhaps your suburb, your favourite beach, your town or your holiday camping ground). Write a draft first and then read it aloud. Change it to achieve good rhyme and rhythm and then write the edited version as your lyric.

4 The chorus makes the main point of any song. It is usually short and often repetitive. Write two choruses, one happy and one unhappy, both dealing with the same subject. You may find the following suggestions helpful.

a Homework Blues **b** Grand Final Fever **c** Teacher's Pet
d Roller Blade Rap **e** Even Best Friends Fight

5 Write a song lyric for children using lots of rhyme and a regular beat. Write it about one of these animals.

a rhinoceros **b** elephant **c** wombat
d koala **e** kangaroo **f** seal

Chapter test

1 Circle the sentence that uses the word *synchronise* correctly.

a We must synchronise our houses. **b** The boys will synchronise their watches.
c Charlie could synchronise his feet tonight.

2 Circle the sentence with the colon correctly placed.

a Mira and Ivan took a picnic lunch: salad, fruit and cold drinks.
b Mira and Ivan: took a picnic lunch, salad, fruit and cold drinks.

3 Circle the correct synonym.

melody: **a** lyric **b** tune **c** chords

CHAPTER 14

Poem

STRUCTURE

title: subject of poem (what it's about)

verses: like paragraphs, they contain different ideas—each one deals with a new aspect of the subject (verse 1—the grace of the heron and daytime verse 2—the darker side of the heron (it is a predator) and night-time

sentences written in groups of images (pictures) over several lines (four images in this one)

The Heron

The heron
like a frail wisp
of smoke glides
down the river canyon,
an arrow
heading for some
unknown place
I see its eye
as big as an egg
the legs like two
silk banners
flying behind
soft soft
the colours and
silent the flight.

Later, in dusk
the hulking shape
just visible
sits still as death
in the fork of a fallen tree
resting
for the journey
into night.

N Stasko

LANGUAGE FEATURES

because the poet wants the reader to share what he/she feels or is experiencing, the language used in poetry appeals to the mind, the heart and the senses

visual images
- *images of heron*
- *change in the light: day to night*

***similes** (like/as comparisons)*

***alliteration** (repetition of the same sound)*

compression of meaning into a single word, e.g. 'arrow' (shape of heron in flight) and 'hulking' (which means hunched over and suggests a threat)

Comprehension

1 Underline the correct answer. A heron is:

a a bat **b** a parrot **c** a water-bird **d** an eagle

2 The heron is flying through a gorge. Is this true or false? ____________________

3 Underline the correct answer. How does the heron fly?

a clumsily **b** gracefully **c** noisily **d** awkwardly

4 The heron flies with its legs tucked under it? Is this true or false? ____________________

5 What is the heron doing at dusk? ____________________

6 What words tell us the heron is grey in colour? ____________________

7 What is meant by *the journey into night*? ____________________

____

8 Its destination is *some unknown place*. To whom is it unknown? ____________________

Writing skills

1 Underline the most relevant answer. This poem has two verses:

a to create a comfortable visual impression **b** to break up the text

c to emphasise the change of mood with evening **d** to change location

2 In the first verse the writer emphasises the graceful flight of the heron. Write two words that suggest this grace.

a ______________________ **b** ______________________

3 In the second verse the poet suggests a darker side to the heron's character. Write two words that suggest this.

a ______________________ **b** ______________________

4 Poets draw pictures with words. These pictures are called **images**. Write down the image Stasko has used to tell us the heron has long, graceful legs. ____

5 In your own words explain what Stasko wants us to see when she describes the heron gliding *like a frail wisp of smoke.* ____

6 Poets use comparisons to make their images more precise and colourful. These comparisons are called **similes**. Similes begin with the words *like* and *as*. Complete the following two similes that are in this poem:

… *its eye as big as* _ _ _ _ _ … and … *sits still as* _ _ _ _ _ …

7 *in the fork of a fallen tree* is an example of al _ _ t _ r _ tion.

8 **a** What sound is repeated throughout verse one? ______________________

b Is this an example of alliteration or a simile? ______________________

9 Underline the correct answer. This sound emphasises:

a the heron's shape **b** the heron's speed **c** the heron's silence

10 How would you describe the tone of this poem?

a descriptive **b** reflective **c** excited

Vocabulary

alliteration	**simile**	**rhythm**	**metaphor**	**image**
atmosphere	**environment**	**journey**	**visible**	**canyon**

1 The words in the top row should be learned carefully. You will use these often in the coming years. They all refer to techniques and tools used by poets.

2 Relate the words in the bottom row to 'The Heron' to understand their meanings. Then break them into syllables for spelling practice, using the Look, Cover, Write, Check method.

Focus on punctuation

Colons and commas

- Colons separate a statement from component activities.
- Commas separate single items in any explanation following a colon, e.g. *All the water birds were there: herons, bitterns, ducks, grebes and ibis.*

Insert colons and commas.

1 Oscar is very talented he sings he dances he juggles.

2 The game plan was simple run on to win play hard to win end up winning.

3 It was a strict regimen the crew followed one man on watch one man asleep one man preparing the next meal one man baling and every two hours each rotated to the next post.

4 In the school Ag. Plot we run a variety of stock lowliner cattle suffolk ewes fat lambs and vealers.

5 My father's pockets were filled with foreign coins francs marks ringgits yen and rupiah.

6 Regulations governing the use of the park no dogs no fires no littering and no alcohol.

7 Harry's shopping list was long nails screws nuts and bolts a pair of pliers screwdrivers and a spanner.

8 Elizabeth considered her options walk comfortably and be late or ride her bike uphill in the heat just to be on time.

Select a word

Using suffixes change these adjectives to nouns.

1 fragile ____________________ **2** agile ____________________

3 sleek ____________________ **4** slender ____________________

5 frail ____________________ **6** weak ____________________

Grammar

Adverbs of manner and degree

- **Adverbs of manner** tell us how something is done, e.g.
  Fred baited the line carefully. Adverb of manner
- **Adverbs of degree** limit the effect of an adjective or of another adverb. They always come in front of that adjective or adverb, e.g.
  He dropped it more accurately than I could have done into the octopus lair. Adverb of degree

1 Match these adverbs to the spaces.

least quietly very relentlessly

a Phillip was ____________________ surprised when he received that award.

b Polly and Sally slipped ____________________ into the back of the room.

c The waves pounded ____________________ on the shore.

d Colin was the ____________________ skilled of all the carpenters.

2 Underline all the adverbs of manner and circle all the adverbs of degree.

a Marjie waited patiently for the right wave and then stylishly surfed it to the beach.

b 'That was a pointlessly mean comment,' her mother said in reproof.

c His father proudly told the neighbours that Mick had done exceptionally well in his exams.

3 The underlined adverbs are labelled. Is each label true or false?

a He fled panic-stricken from the scene. Adverb of manner ____________________

b Nonchalantly she strolled past and ignored him. Adverb of manner ____________________

c The punishment was <u>unnecessarily</u> severe. Adverb of manner ______________________

d His invitation was <u>happily</u> accepted. Adverb of degree ______________________

Word study

Alliteration is the grouping together of words that begin with the same sound or are close to each other; e.g.

five fat felines

He fidgeted, froze and fidgeted some more as he waited at the bus stop.

1 Underline the alliteration in each of these.

a Dandelions danced in the breeze.

b The snake slid slowly and silently over the step and onto the grass.

c Forty-five firemen fought the ferocious warehouse blaze.

d A series of silly slogans appeared on the steel wall.

2 Insert a word from the vocabulary list in the following sentence.

a The mist was so thick the Harbour Bridge was not ______________________.

b If you set out on a *journey* would you be more likely to take hours or days to complete it? ____________

c Insert the missing letters. If you set out on a *sea journey*, you would be going on a v _ _ _ _ e.

d Select a word from the vocabulary list and add a prefix to create an **antonym** (word opposite in meaning) to complete the following.

If you are not visible you are _ _ _ _ _ _ _ _ _ _ .

3 By using **affixes** (prefixes and/or suffixes) write antonyms for the following.

a cheerful ______________________ **b** allow ______________________

c necessary ______________________ **d** known ______________________

e graceful ______________________ **f** ordered ______________________

4 We understand the meanings of words in context. When we select a word we must consider the context in which we intend to use it. Words may have the same general meaning but belong in different contexts.

a The word *frail* has three synonyms below. Underline them.

i fragile **ii** slender **iii** brittle **iv** robust **v** old **vi** weak **vii** threadbare

b However, even though they all mean the same thing, they don't all describe the same situations. Underline the correct alternatives in the following.

i A weak/frail old dog can still dig up the garden when he is bored.

ii The frail/fragile china ornament was blown over and smashed.

iii Very old letters are usually fragile/brittle with age.

iv After a long battle with pneumonia Uncle Jim is too weak/frail to walk unaided.

5 By using prefixes, write antonyms (opposites) for the following.

a happy ______________________ **b** cued ______________________

c furred ______________________ **d** reliable ______________________

e agreeable ______________________ **f** read ______________________

Evaluating other people's writing

1 This was meant to be a rhyming poem. Can you find rhymes to fill the rhyme spaces?

A bearded dragon
basked in the sun.
'Such fun' said the dragon
I don't want to r _ _.'

'I wish I were a shingle back
I'd never have to hurry
just amble slowly across the tr _ _ _
and take my time without a fl _ _ _ _.'

2 **Wet Day Routine**

Smelly joggers, soaking clothes
Steamy windows and soggy carpet.
Students talk, teachers rouse
Pens won't write on damp pages.
The clock ticks and Simon coughs
Kylie copies, Mark dobs.
Three bells ring
Wet weather rules.
Crowded corridors, squashed bags,
Sit down, shut up.
Mark gets his, Kylie's a sneak.

a Underline all the poetic techniques this student has used.

i alliteration **ii** similes **iii** visual images **iv** auditory images

b Good poetry uses the senses. Underline the senses this student has used.

i sight **ii** hearing **iii** touch **iv** taste **v** smell

c In the second line what punctuation mark could have replaced *and*? ____________________

d Read aloud lines 3 and 4. If the student had written *pages damp* he would have maintained a regular rhythm/rhyme and improved his poem. Underline the correct word.

Word usage

A **metaphor** is a kind of comparison in which the similarity is so close that one thing is called by the name of another. Children use metaphors all the time without knowing it. When one girl calls another a *pig*, she doesn't mean she has grown a snout or a curly tail. She simply means she is behaving like a pig. Many metaphors are part of everyday language.

1 Underline the metaphors in the following.

a I keep the good china out of Andrew's way. He's a bull in a china shop.

b The sergeant is a real snake in the grass. Don't tell him anything.

c If I tell the Principal what I suspect it will really put a cat among the pigeons.

2 Match the metaphors in question 1 with the following meanings.

a cause an uproar ____________________

b he is clumsy ____________________

c he is untrustworthy and deceitful ____________________

3 Write the appropriate metaphor in the space.

clouds face space eyes

The sky's ______________ darkened, scowled and began a low mutter of anger on the horizon.

4 What is the metaphor in this sentence?

A grass fire spilled over the ridge and ran in fiery rivulets down the slope along the lines of tussock grass to gather in a wash of flame in the heavily wooded gully at the bottom.

a water flow **b** rain **c** flame

5 **Onomatopoeia** is using words that sound like the action they represent, e.g. *The cat meowed, the frog croaked*. Supply onomatopoeic verbs for these sentences.

a The snake h _ _ _ _ d as it reared up in fright.

b The coins cl _ _ _ _ d in the jar.

c Wolves were h _ _ _ _ _ g in the moonlight.

d Bells c _ _ _ _ d in the distance.

e Edgily the dogs g _ _ _ _ _ d at each other.

Quick think

1 Many well-known sayings are similes. Write down similes that mean the following, e.g. *very poor = as poor as a church mouse.*

a very proud ____________________

b very happy ____________________

c very sly ____________________

d very brave ____________________

2 Fit these people and places of history and myth to their well-known similes.
Hercules, Croesus, Hades, Attila the Hun

a as rich as ____________________

b as dark as ____________________

c as strong as ____________________

d as barbaric as ____________________

Idiom

Explain:

1 As the ship sank, the man who could not swim was between the devil and the deep blue sea. ____________________

2 A dentist's appointment on my birthday! That's a real fly in the ointment. ____________________

Writing paragraphs and whole texts

1 Try your hand at some two-line poems using a simile. (Remember: similes begin with *like* or *as*.)

a The traffic moved off ____________ **b** Skateboarders hurtled down ____________ **c** The moon rose over the city ____________

2 Try alliterative descriptions of animals, e.g.

Chattering chooks chase and chivvy chickens.

a cat ____________

b monkey ____________

c fish ____________

3 Now try onomatopoeic descriptions, e.g.

thundering, trumpeting, squealing herd of elephants

a ____________ alley cat

b ____________ classroom

c ____________ railway pigeons

4 Write a word in the space that rhymes with the last word of the first line.

a Purring contentedly on the mat
lay my mother's fat spoiled ______.

b Undeterred, the terrier yapped
for all that I coaxed and cl _ _ _ _ _ .

5 This poem has six five-beat lines. It relies on its regular rhythm for appeal. Try writing a farm or a sea poem on the same pattern.

In the deep of night ____________
when the moon rides high ____________
the little black bats ____________
are out and about— ____________
to dance under stars ____________
and dine on the wing. ____________

6 **Haiku** are three-line poems containing a single image, e.g.

Iron autumn
And all the cold wind-bells
Tinkling.
(*poet unknown*)

In the streets
Small boys and skateboards
Dice with Death.
(*anonymous*)

Add second and third lines to each of these first lines.

a At the social ____________ ____________

b Doing homework ____________ ____________

c Summer ____________ ____________

7 Read aloud the following English poem. Then try to write a similar poem for Australians.

Afternoons	**Afternoons**
Prodigal summer afternoons	______________________________
Buzz and shrill, shimmering bright;	______________________________
Brooding afternoons in winter	______________________________
Muffle sound and hoard the light.	______________________________
(unknown English poet)	

Chapter test

1 Circle the correct answer. The underlined words in this sentence are:

a a metaphor **b** a simile

Lightning flashed <u>its forked tongue</u> across the sky.

2 Circle the onomatopoeic word in this sentence.

Single raindrops pinged on the metal roof.

3 Complete this sentence.

Seven silly sailors is an example of ______________________

4 Underline the adverb of degree in this sentence.

Elephants eat much more than rabbits.

5 Which sentence is correctly punctuated?

a He checked the equipment, paint, brush, drop mat, step ladder and rag. It was all there.

b He checked the equipment: paint, brush, drop mat, step ladder and rag. It was all there.

CHAPTER 15

Television review

STRUCTURE

title of regular review column

program name and screening details

introduction: *lead-in sentence sets pattern of negative review (it's the fault of the video camera)*

body of review: *each paragraph deals with one negative aspect of the show (poor film, poor narrator, poor script)*

conclusion: *sums up reviewer's negative reaction to program*

Gerri Sutton's View

World's wildest police videos

Channel 10, 7.30 pm

How much we have the video camera to thank for. Due to the proliferation of these hand-held spy machines and the gaping maws of television networks, there's a constant supply of images of precocious kids, performing pets and men with big bellies seeking their fifteen seconds of fame.

It's irksome stuff, but it pales beside the dross featured in this series, car chase after car chase, so poorly filmed much of it looks like a pirate video game. Surely only the most rabid rubberneck would find entertainment in grainy videos from Arkansas, Indiana, Michigan or Milledgeville, Georgia.

Adding insult to the occasional injury is John Bunnell, with his motionless coiffure, who hollers rather than narrates, maintaining an air of hyper-hysteria as he bellows about running from the 'lah' and cops in 'pursoot', 'cuff 'im ... take 'im down!'

The only time the smoothly tanned Bunnell's enthusiasm for car chases is surpassed is when he discusses muddy security footage of a couple of snatch-and-grabs.

But his finest moment comes when he voice-overs incongruously inserted film of Indonesian riots, in which well-armoured police beat unarmed protesters. According to Bunnell, regardless of their politics they are just doing their jobs: they have 'saved the paradise of Indonesia from becoming paradise lost'.

And why are we being served up this compost as entertainment? Ask Bunnell. 'For one reason, knowledge is power and power may save your life.'

Perhaps, but it didn't save me from a Bunnell of a headache.

Who Weekly

LANGUAGE FEATURES

strong images

repetition of examples

compression of meaning into single verbs

direct quotation

use of ***satire****; this is* *not* *his finest moment*

negative nouns

sarcasm (turns Bunnell's own words against him)

*C*omprehension

1 What two things does Sutton blame for the poorly filmed, cheap television shows we see?

____

2 Underline the correct answer. A *rabid rubberneck* is a person who in his viewing habits is:

a irrational **b** indiscriminate **c** fidgety **d** annoyingly talkative

3 *it pales beside the dross. Dross* in this context means

a metallic scum **b** rubbish **c** film **d** performing pets

4 Bunnell is an asset to this program in Sutton's opinion. Is this true or false? ______

5 Did Bunnell film the Indonesian riots himself ? ______
What words tell you this? ______

6 What evidence does the reviewer offer to suggest that most of the film footage is American?

______

7 Quote two words from the review that tell us Sutton considers this program rubbish.

______ ______

8 The words *muddy footage* refer to:
a mud-damaged film **b** the reporter's muddy footwear **c** blurred, unclear film

9 The term *snatch-and-grabs* refers to:
a film taken on the run **b** thefts **c** minor assaults

Writing skills

1 What tells us at first glance that this is a TV review? ______

2 What phrase conveys Sutton's dislike of video cameras? ______

3 The comment *Adding insult to the occasional injury* is based on a well-known:
a antonym **b** metaphor **c** cliché **d** simile

4 *Gaping maws* is an image more usually applied to what sea creature? ______

5 What does this image tell us about television networks? ______

6 What verb first confirms that Bunnell himself is an American? ______

7 Underline the correct answer. Sutton quotes Bunnell directly in words like *lah* (law) and *pursoot* (pursuit). This sort of quotation is:
a careful reporting for accuracy's sake **b** careful reporting with the intent to mock
c careful reporting to validate Sutton's claim to familiarity with the series

8 Underline the correct answer. The phrase *finest moment* as used in this review is an example of:
a satire **b** irony **c** simple statement **d** humour

9 Look back through the review. Find two adjectives that negatively describe the quality of the film footage in this series. ______ ______

10 How does Sutton twist Bunnell's justification of his show to criticise it? ______

______

11 Could this be described as a balanced review? Explain your answer. ______

______

Vocabulary

rabid	bellies	precocious	enthusiasm	surpass
shrieked	delicious	thunder	melodious	whispered

1 Underline the adjectival suffix *~ious*, where it occurs. This is a very common suffix.

2 Circle the 'ie' spelling pattern of *shrieked*. Memorise using the Look, Cover, Write, Check method.

Focus on punctuation

Punctuation marks

1 Insert capitals, question marks, exclamation marks, full stops and inverted commas.

a was john curtin prime minister during the second world war

b dr john flynn established the flying doctor service in the outback

c i won i won he shouted waving his lottery ticket

2 Insert commas, apostrophes and dashes.

a Julio Bruno and Ben were all driven by Brunos father

b I borrowed your Human Nature CD sorry I forgot to ask for the loan of it

c I beat Micks dog to the corner in two minutes flat Micks still getting there

3 Insert colons, semicolons and commas.

a The following dignitaries were present the Mayor the Town Clerk the local clergy and Mr Kwong a well-known and respected philanthropist.

b He ate his meal quickly he had a train to catch.

Select a word

Insert the correct answer.

1 the singular of *bellies* ____________________

2 the plural of *supply* ____________________

2 the singular of *fillies* ____________________

4 the plural of *misery* ____________________

5 the singular of *allies* ____________________

6 the plural of *enemy* ____________________

Grammar

Adverbs of time and place

- **Adverbs of time** tell us when an action happens, e.g.
  He left afterwards.
- **Adverbs of place** tell us where it happens, e.g.
  The book is there on the top shelf.

1 Underline the adverbs of time in the following.

a A year later he succeeded.

b Six months ago he went overseas.

c Sometimes all my cousins visit at once.

d We never travel together in case of an accident.

2 Underline the adverbs of place in the following

a We looked everywhere but could not find the wallet.

b It was nowhere to be seen.

c John said it could be anywhere.

d Far below we could see tiny starfish.

3 Insert an appropriate adverb as indicated.

a That lost dog could be __________ by now. (place)

b It only rains in the desert __________. (time)

c Leave these here and put those __________. (place)

d __________ after rain we see a rainbow. (time)

Word study

1 Replace each underlined word with a word from the bottom row of the vocabulary list.

a John said, 'Sssh. I hear someone coming.' ______________________

b The sound of the surf could be heard before we reached the beach. ______________________

c We ate a nice Indonesian meal. ______________________

d The choir at the Jacaranda Festival was very nice. ______________________

e Julia said, 'I can't bear the sound of nails on a blackboard.' ______________________

2 Insert words from top row of the vocabulary list in the blanks.

a The team were encouraged by the ______________________ of their fans.

b Con is a ______________________ supporter of the Sydney Swans.

c Mark Taylor chose not to ______________________ Don Bradman's Australian record of 334 runs in a Test match.

3 Find synonyms in the list for these words.

a excel ______________ **b** fanatical ______________

c keenness ______________ **d** screeched ______________

e tuneful ______________ **f** tasty ______________

4 Find antonyms in the list for these words.

a tuneless ______________ **b** murmured ______________

c repulsive ______________ **d** balanced ______________

e shouted ______________ **f** boredom ______________

Evaluating other people's writing

The Bad Side

There's lots of shows on TV about bad mean guys today. I reckon we need more shows like *Home and Away* and *Sea Patrol*. theyre all about real people that do things like we do like getting into trouble and getting it sorted out and stuff. I mean, what's to enjoy about dudes beating up other dudes when they don't get cort? You want them to get paid back for what they done. *Sea Patrol* is great. You learn all about the navy and what they do and what its like on a patrol boat and how everyone has to cooprate to get a job done and there's always a bit of adventure or a bit of romance and things like that. I'm going to join the navy when I leave school.

1 Circle any of these elements you consider missing from this review.

a reviewer's opinion of one show **b** details of title and screening time

c reference to the show's main characters **d** reference to plot and dialogue

e reference to setting and costume **f** comment on likely audience appeal

2 This text would be correctly described as:

a a narrative **b** an instruction **c** an opinion **d** a review

3 Which of these apply to the second sentence?

a It is correctly punctuated.
b It uses inappropriate colloquial language.
c It is too long.
d It contains specific evidence for its opinion.

4 Circle any of these words from the text that are inappropriate in a review.

a dude
b mean
c romance
d stuff
e adventure
f reckon

5 These occur in the text. Write them in the spaces provided.

a two misspelt words ____________________ ____________________
b a verb that does not agree in number with its subject ____________________
c an irrelevant statement ____
d one grammatically incorrect verb ____________________

6 Underline the meaningless words in these extracts from the text.

a *getting into trouble and getting it sorted out and stuff*
b *a bit of adventure or a bit of romance and things like that*
c *I mean, what's to enjoy about*

Word usage

1 Underline the correct homonym.

a We camped their/there overnight.
b There/They're the last rations we have.
c Where their/they're/there are rabbits there/their/they're will always be eagles.
d Were/We're going ice-skating.
e Where/Were is that man running?
f The thieves we're/were caught in the act.

2 We walk differently in different situations. We use different verbs for different walks. Choose the most appropriate verb from the words below and insert them in the following. (You may need to adjust for tense.)

trudge shuffle limp stride amble

a Charlie ____________________________ home an hour after the cross-country winner was declared.
b Nicole and her dog liked to ____________________________ by the river.
c Dragging his shattered leg the soldier ____________________________ into camp.
d The twins ____________________________ their toes in the dust and laughed.
e ____________________________ out proudly to receive that award—you have earned it.

3 Exactly how big is *big*? Choose a *big* adjective from the list to fit the space.

enormous large gigantic colossal

a Horses are _______________ animals compared to sheep.
b A _____________ crane carried timber to the sixtieth floor.
c The placid blue whale is an _________________ animal.
d The brontosaur weighed a _____________ thirty tons.

4 And how small is *small*? Choose a *small* adjective from the list to fit the space.

small tiny microscopic minute

a Bacteria are ________________ organisms.

b The pony is a ______________ horse.

c A skink is _____________ compared to a goanna.

d A miniature is a ____________ painting worn inside a locket.

Quick think

1 Find words in the 'World's wildest police videos' text to mean:

a irritating ____________________________ **b** rubbish ____________________________

c fanatical ____________________________ **d** hairstyle ____________________________

e film clips ____________________________

2 The prefix *hyper~* means excessively beyond or above what is normal. Complete the following.

a a huge supermarket is a hyper _ _ _ _

b Gerri Sutton accuses Bunnell of hyper- _ _ _ _ _ _ _ _

c to be excessively critical is to be hyper _ _ _ _ _ _ _ _

d very high blood pressure is called hyper _ _ _ _ _ _ _

e a very energetic child is sometimes called hyper _ _ _ _ _ _

3 The prefix *micro~* means very, very small. Complete the following.

a A magnifying tool for seeing bacteria and smaller life forms is a micros _ _ _ e.

b A manager who looks after tiny details is a microm _ _ _ _ _ r.

c Our view of the world of a minute form of life is a microc _ _ m.

d A tiny form of life such as a virus is a micro-o _ _ _ _ _ _ m.

e The tiny Australian black bat is a microb _ t.

Idiom

Explain:

1 I'm out of my depth in this maths class. ____________________________

____

2 When I came first in English I was stoked. ____________________________

____

Writing paragraphs and whole texts

1 Using the words and phrases below, complete the following comment on the ratings success of the TV series *Seachange*.

risk, base, *The Man From Snowy River*, early, unknown, screen, pleased, Starring, producer, reception, followers, often, star, series, ratings a ______________ Sigrid Thornton, this series had an automatic ratings b ______________ before it reached the c ______________. Her loyal band of d ______________, won in films such as e ______________ ______________ and f ______________ such as 'All the Rivers Run', were only too g ______________ to see her again. Fans such as these are prepared to stay with the h ______________ shaky i ______________ days of a new series for the sake of their j ______________. Such a k ______________ base means the l ______________ of a new series can m ______________ taking longer to find favourable n ______________ than the one who is introducing a series with a screen o ______________.

2 Match an appropriate description in Column B with an aspect of TV drama production in Column A.

Column A		**Column B**
a subject	______	**i** meticulously scripted
b theme	______	**ii** period
c characters	______	**iii** hauntingly lyrical
d sets	______	**iv** gloomy
e dialogue	______	**v** murder and betrayal
f costume	______	**vi** individual responsibility
g soundtrack	______	**vii** shadowed and flickering
h camera work	______	**viii** complex and ruthless
i lighting	______	**ix** close-up and confronting
j atmosphere	______	**x** authentic

3 Write a brief positive review of a new TV science fiction series called *Black Hole* using phrases from the list below. The first sentence is done for you.

- well-developed characters
- spectacular special effects
- glamorous costumes
- action-packed drama
- chillingly believable space stations

Everything about 'Black Hole' appeals to a true sci-fi fan. ______________________________

____

____

____

____

____

____

____

4 Write a brief negative review of the same series using phrases from the list below. The first sentence is done for you.

- usual science fiction special effects
- cheap glitz
- bizarre characters
- rather tacky sets
- erratic plot and confusing chronology of events

All true sci-fi fans will be disappointed with 'Black Hole'. ____________________

____

____

____

____

____

____

____

____

____

____

5 Write a six-line review of your favourite television show.

____

____

____

____

____

____

Chapter test

1 Circle the adverb in this sentence.

We never swim outside the flags.

2 The underlined adverb tells us where my ball went. True/False

His ball went <u>further</u> than mine.

3 Correct the misspelt word in this sentence.

Our supplys were late arriving. ______________

4 Correct the misspelt word in this sentence.

The fish in black bean sauce was delishus. ______________

5 Circle the correct word in this sentence.

Were/We're/Where starting our holidays tomorrow.

ANSWER SECTION

CHAPTER 1: CARTOON

Comprehension

1 false
2 b
3 Wal did not clear the drain. He crashed in it.
4 c
5 It is The Dog's story being told.

Writing skills

1 text, illustration
2 a, c, d
3 The first text suggests uncertainty and the second text suggests certainty.
4 scene, story, conclusion
5 b
6 expressions
7 The illustration shows the dust of speed riding and the text is written in a large bold type with an exclamation mark.
8 b
9 d
10 c

Focus on punctuation

1 **a** When the Principal, Mrs Taylor, arrives, tell her Mrs Jones called.
b Even though he is twenty, Peter does not have a driving licence.
c Feroza's Meats is an excellent butcher shop.
d John's father runs a carpentry workshop called Woodchips.
e Although Brompton High School faces Lyons Road its entry is on Miller Street.
2 **a** James Jones travelled to Cairns.
b Rev. John Hales conducted a service.
c Maj. Henry Lewis is in charge of supplies.
d The Hon. John Howard is a former prime minister of Australia.
e The South Seas Fishing Coop. has gone bankrupt.

Select a word

1 portrait
2 illustration
3 humorous
4 diagram
5 text
6 dialogue

Grammar

1 **a** Judy Horacek and Cathy Wilcox are well-known Australian cartoonists.
b Michael Leunig, the Victorian cartoonist, has had several books published.
c Larson is a much-loved American cartoonist.
d Some cartoonists go on to make animated films like *Happy Feet*.
e Some films about an animated character are set in the real world.
2 **a** F **b** S
c S **d** F
e F **f** F
g S

3 **a** Ginger Meggs, Australia's, characters
b Cartoons, prime minister, Paul Keating, undertaker
c Caricatures, features, eyebrows
d Animators, Road Runner, Bugs Bunny, Mickey Mouse
e cartoonists, ideas, sketches, detail
4 **a** abstract
b i abstract ii abstract
c concrete
d i concrete ii abstract

Word study

1 **a** humorous
b cartoonist, text
c frame
d portrait, caricature
e diagram, illustration
f commentator
2 **a** diagram
b commentator
c dialogue
d illustration

Word usage

1 **a** reinforcements **b** fought
c adjacent **d** quench
e ancient **f** external
2 **a** horsehair **b** impressive
3 **a** ancient
b collapsed
c remains
4 **a** major **b** brigade
c remains **d** external

Quick think
1 – b, **2** – e, **3** – a, **4** – c, **5** – d

Proofreading
All major newspapers carry cartoons of two kinds, humorous and social comment. Each paper has its own cartoonists who produce cartoons about current issues; e.g. Cathy Wilcox, whose cartoons appear in the *Sydney Morning Herald*. Sometimes people are offended by the way a cartoonist has shown them and in this case they may ask a lawyer for help. However, most people take cartoons in a spirit of fun.

Idiom
1 What you don't have always seems better or more exciting than what you do have.
2 When problems appear they are never minor troubles.

Writing paragraphs and whole texts
1 Original text read:
- frame 1—Life gets rather tedious around here sometimes
- frame 2—Same old routine, day in day out
- frame 3—DINNER, FRED. But then again, some old routines do have their moments!

2 Your answer should talk about how everyone contributes to pollution levels and should act to reduce his or her own contributions to it.

Chapter test
1 d **2** c

CHAPTER 2: DIARY ENTRY

Comprehension
1 mother's
2 b
3 b
4 the cat
5 Ed is quiet and pleasant with his father, but cross and loud with James.
6 nurse
7 The immediate problem is the dirty socks.
8 James's real problem is that Ed is taking his mother's place.

Writing skills
1 to date entry for future reference
2 a
3 He tells what he is doing now, and then what happened before this.
4 b
5 Steam only blasts under pressure and Ed feels under pressure.
6 b
7 angel halo
8 third last sentence in para. 5
9 a
10 Last paragraph because it reveals how hard James has found life without his mother.
11 b, f, h
12 e

Focus on punctuation
1 H.J. Adams Pty Ltd has expanded its premises.
2 Rev. John Flynn established the Flying Doctor Service.
3 Capt. James Cook's ship was the *Endeavour*.
4 Ed was just in one of those moods.
5 She gained her BSc/B.Sc. from Sydney University.
6 I wrote to Mr and Mrs Georgiou last night.
7 Benbow and Assocs have just merged with Brierley and Co. to their mutual advantage.
8 Gov. Gen. Sir Ninian Stephen later assisted with peace talks in Northern Ireland.

Select a word
1 complete
2 patient
3 argue
4 hoping
5 probably
6 laundry

Grammar
1 **a** A cartoonist illustrates and writes text.
b Leunig works in Melbourne but Wilcox works in Sydney.
c Franz is a German migrant and his wife Heidi comes from Austria.
d Franz goes out to work but/and Heidi works at home.
e Heidi may stay at home but she is not a shy person.

2 **a** so **b** so
c then **d** so
e but **f** but

Word study
1 hygienic
2 ie
3 **a** believe
b retrieve
c achieve
d conceive
4 **a** receipt
b deceive
c receiver
5 a, c, d

Word usage
1 shouldn't, through, teasing, to know, out, have, any more, value
2 **a** practising
b bought
c practice
d brought
3 **a** stationery
b licence
c aggravate
d dear
e stationary

4 **a** practice
b practice
c brought
d practise
e hung
f hanged

Quick think

1 litter
2 pod
3 pride
4 mob
5 pack
6 troop
7 flight
8 shoal
9 school
10 gaggle

Proofreading

retrieve, believe, hygienic, deceived, believe, relieved, receipt

Idiom

1 Susan will be in trouble at home tonight.
2 He looked very pleased and satisfied.

Chapter test

1 so
2 b

CHAPTER 3: PERSONAL LETTER

Comprehension

1 b
2 yes; one month's notice
3 c
4 She is changing her plans so she can attend a family party.
5 Very well. They even know each other's viewing habits.
6 b
7 Call me on the telephone
8 b
9 flat or unit 4 at 67 Fifield Lane

Writing skills

1 c
2 Dear Dr Ibrahim
3 d
4 It is not a formal word but a colloquial (everyday) expression.
5 b, d
6 **a** a bit rough
b on the go
7 a
8 a
9 d

Focus on punctuation

Australians come from many different races and cultures but they are one people. Australians celebrate this fact on Australia day on January 26 in a uniquely Australian way. Local communities gather together around a barbecue to celebrate being Australian and to honour those people who have helped improve the lives of their fellow citizens.

Select a word

1 address	2 information
3 inquiry	4 salutation
5 address	6 margin

Grammar

1 **a** unless
b when
c although
d because
e although
2 **a** and
b and, but
c then
d so
3 **a** He won but he did not win fairly.
b Enzo can swing on a trapeze and he can also walk a tightrope.
c Rain is pouring down so the washing will not dry.
d The sheep ate the grass and they ate all the flowers in the garden.
4 **a** If/because the train is late we will catch a bus.
b As/when/after/because the ferry drifted from the wharf a passenger fell into the water.
c We would like to go for a walk but it is raining.
d If you are bitten by a snake, bandage the site firmly and see a doctor.

Word study

1 **a** address
b recipient
c complaint
d greeting or salutation
e information
2 **a** addressee
b lessee
c amputee
3 **a** exultation
b circulation
c transportation
d conservation
e reservation
f rotation
g recreation
h innovation

Word usage

1 **a** 33 Great North Road
Abbotsford
NSW 2046
b Dear Jason
c Dear Mr Bowden

2 **a** F **b** T
c F **d** T
e T
3 **a** – iii, **b** – i, **c** – iv, **d** – ii
4 **a** C **b** F
c C **d** F

Quick think

1 **a** ophthalmologist
b seismologist
c biologist
d vulcanologist
e geologist
2 **a** misanthropist
b terrorist
c antagonist
d misogynist

Proofreading

recipient, inquiry, salutation, signature, address

Idiom

1. That child is very active today.
2. Don't make excuses.

Writing paragraphs and whole texts

1 **a** 1
b 2
c 1
d 2
e 1
f 3
g 3
h 3

2
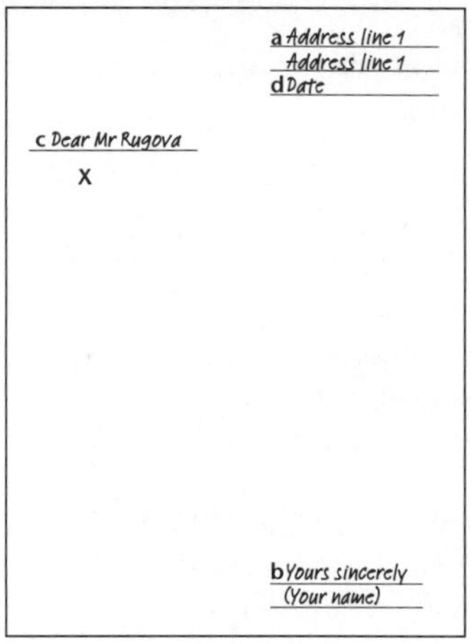

Chapter test

1 because
2 Clinton hit the ball for six but no one saw it. They were all watching the snake on the pitch.

CHAPTER 4: FACTUAL RECOUNT

Comprehension

1 b
2 Sara Reynolds
3 c
4 a
5 She protects, cleans and plays with them.
6 Because they need frequent feeding.
7 She barks and climbs into the car too.
8 c
9 c

Writing skills

1 It includes origin of story and has very short paragraphs.
2 contrast
3 It is not a legal adoption.
4 Ellie is a human name and so it could refer to a woman or a dog.
5 b
6 taking the place of the rabbits' real mother
7 a
8 The dog and rabbits are of different species.
9 b
10 c

Focus on punctuation

1 John cried out, 'Where's my skateboard?'
2 The Kelly gang robbed the Braidwood bank and escaped shouting 'You won't catch us!'
3 'Boom!' sounded the great cannon at midday.
4 Capt. Henry Matson asked if the third watch had been relieved.
5 Harvey hissed 'Don't move! There's a snake next to your foot.'
6 'Watch out!' the rigger shouted as the beam crashed to the footpath.
7 'Man overboard!' The cry ran the length of the ship.
8 Why are all the clocks stopped at 10.45?
9 His Royal Highness, Prince Fergus George, shouted 'Off with his head!'

Select a word

1 sorrow
2 anxiety
3 pity
4 excitement
5 concentration
6 anticipation

Grammar

1 **a** !
b !
c ?
d ?
e !
2 **a** Q
b E
c E
d E
3 **a** . I
b ? D
c . I
d . I

Word study

1 **a** empathy
b excitement
c sorrow
d sympathy
e concentration
f pity
g envy
h anxiety
i anticipation

2 **a** concentration
b anxiety
c pity
d excitement
3 **a** anticipation
b empathy
c excitement
d anxiety

Evaluating other people's writing

1 fact of two different species
2 rabbits at school because of feeding demands

Word usage

1 **a** kits
b calves
c joeys
d cubs
e goslings
f pups
2 **a** rear
b surrogate
c community
d solitary
e flock
3 **a** sorrow
b envy
c anxiety
d anticipation
e jealous

Quick think

1 **a** lender
b child
c pudding
d nine
e cooks
f fall
2 **a** e **b** b
c f **d** c
e d **f** a

Proofreading

In old Australia orphan lambs were raised in a wooden box with a hole in the side. Outside the box a ewe whose own lamb had died was short-tethered to a post close to the box hole. She could hear the lamb's sad cry, 'baa baa', but could not see it. The lamb could put its head through the hole, find the sheep's udder and drink. Even though sheep do not accept lambs that are not their own, in this way an orphan lamb could be saved.

Idiom

1 James: You are a very long time coming.
2 Hurry up.

Writing paragraphs and whole texts

2 **a** Billie Piper's tour cancelled
b Billie Piper, 16-year-old British popstar
c Billie Piper voiceless with virus
d Confined to hotel room
e In Australia to promote 'Honey to the Bee' single
f Billie Piper regrets cancellation
g Billie Piper missed Grand Hyatt performance
h Billie Piper to miss Mount Druitt appearance today

Chapter test

1 d
2 d

CHAPTER 5: NARRATIVE

Comprehension

1 d
2 true
3 his bravery
4 A *cliff* is a steep slope going a long way down to the water level.
5 Felix was under water longer than it takes to drown.
6 Something in the experience underwater gave him confidence and superhuman strength.

Writing skills

1 all the way to the centre of the earth
2 a
3 **a** cliff
b indirect description
4 para. 1
5 He wore swimming trunks to school under his uniform.
6 d
7 shot
8 last sentence
9 a, c
10 a
11 small, has a brother and a sister, lacks confidence, of school age
12 events and incidents

Focus on punctuation

1 **a** The chips were shared among Elise, Simone, Raelene and Katie.
b Unless every Tom, Dick and Harry comes there will be no audience.
c Pack a towel, swimmers, sunscreen, a hat and some mosquito repellent.
d The feline species includes domestic cats, lions, tigers, leopards, cheetahs, cougars, jaguars, civets and various smaller forest dwelling cats.
2 **a** 'Clean your shoes, find a handkerchief, put on a jumper and don't be late for school,' Mum says every morning.
b Run a length of track, swim an expanse of water, cycle a stretch of road—they're the three parts of a triathlon.
c The old Greek Olympic Games only featured running, hurdling, wrestling, leaping, discus and javelin throwing and long jump.
d Carving bone, whittling wood, polishing gems and sculpting stone are ancient skills.
3 **a** ✗ **b** ✗
c ✓ **d** ✗

Select a word

1 deceive, agitate, damage, escape
2 a scarlet
 b crimson
 c vermilion
 d burgundy
3 a stroll
 b amble
 c meander
 d wander

Grammar

1 a won
 b trains
2 a ruffled
 b closed, inhaled, jumped
 c was, looked
3 a had walked
 b had been identified, surrendered
 c is, will go
4 a will play, recovers
 b will be
 c has been removed, built
 d am, to see, come
 e were, broke

Word study

1 a narrate, relate
 b inhale, exhale
 c quarry
 d slightest
 e rigid
2 a rigid
 b exhale
 c inhale
 d quarry
 e suggest
3 a retell
 b exhale
4 a prey
 b ii

Word usage

1 a unpleasant, not, an
 b ii
 c He sat down on his usual chair.
 d He ate rice bubbles and toast and drank milk.
 e suddenly
 f Henry
2 a screeched
 b snarls
 c chatter
 d bellowed
 e whimpered

Quick think

1 reapply
2 rewrite
3 redefine
4 exhale
5 extrovert
6 exclude
7 inhale
8 introvert
9 include

Proofreading

1 Peter Nye was elected school captain.
2 Maria Kwok has been nominated Citizen of the Year.
3 Yang Brothers is a carpet-laying service.
4 The Fred Hollows Foundation helps restore the sight of blind people in Asia, Africa and Australia.

Idiom

1 Lucy had two options and both were very unpleasant.
2 Supervision is necessary.

Writing paragraphs and whole texts

1 a ii, iii, i, iv
 b iii, vii, ii, iv, vi, v, i, viii
 c ii, iii, i, iv
2 e, c, d, b, f, j, g, h, i, a

Chapter test

1 peeled
2 a
3 applesX

CHAPTER 6: INTERVIEW

Comprehension

1 false
2 b
3 c
4 false
5 b
6 b
7 She learns from problems rather than is disappointed by them.

Writing skills

1 a, c
2 public/sporting, private/family
3 c
4 b
5 sympathetic
6 transcript
7 interviewer
8 b
9 colloquial
10 It ends the interview on a happy/laughing note.

Focus on punctuation

1 a Builders are responsible for the laying of the foundations, the erection of the frame, the roofing of the frame, the cladding of the walls and the fitting out of the house.
 b The Eora, who lived in the Sydney area when the Europeans arrived, suffered terribly from the smallpox brought by the newcomers.

c In one hectic day Peter went to school, had cricket training, fitted in his letterbox leafleting job, debated with his school team and came home to do homework.
d The spy passed his information to his counterpart, the undersecretary at the Rugovian Embassy.
e Jackie Chan, an Australian from Canberra, is an international film star.

2 a On the other side of the creek, near the apple gums, a horse grazed contentedly.
b Mario, my father's brother, the man who runs the garden nursery, is also a vintner.
c Dollarbirds, the ones with small pale coin spots under their wings, are migratory.
d Woodworkers, carpenters, joiners and furniture makers need good quality tools.

3 d

Select a word
1 serious
2 valuable
3 favourite
4 competitive
5 communicate
6 practice

Grammar
1 a, b, c, d, f, g, i, j
2 a ate, ran, talked, spoke
b i They planned to go bowling.
ii We chose to avoid city traffic.
iii Michaela went ice-skating on Saturday.
iv Triathletes ran, swam, and cycled long distances.
3 a Dilip dives in the deep end.
b My brother loves that picture.
c Chloe drinks all the lemonade.
d The tiger cub laps water
4 past

Word study
1 a competitive
b favourite
c serious
d communicate
2 a practise
b practice
c practice
d practise
3 a read
b herd
c wrings, ring
d bread
e creek, creak
4 a flea
b past
c loan
d whole

Evaluating other people's writing
1 no
2 a, b, c, d
3 c
4 a, c, d

Word usage
1 a attention
b communicate
c valuable
d unproductive
2 a yes
b no
c yes
3 a Your Excellency
b Your Grace
c Your Majesty
d Sir/Madam (Ma'am)
e Mr/Madam President

Quick think
1 sob
2 asserted
3 plummet
4 soak
5 demand
6 slash
7 devour
8 trudge
9 pummelled
10 scold

Proofreading
Olivia leaned over the gate and looked down Trinculo Road. There was nothing to be seen except an ancient truck and two men unloading fruit crates. She sighed and idly swung on the gate while she contemplated whether to go looking for Ming Lee in the library or down among the CD racks in Tony's Music House.

Idiom
1 Watch this situation.
2 The rain was very heavy.

Writing paragraphs and whole texts
1 a i How long have you been playing football?
ii When did you first play for Souths?
iii How do you feel about being called *the new face of football*?
iv Is it true that you have been considering a switch to Rugby Union?
b Q There is a rumour around that you might switch to Rugby Union. Is that true?
A Well, I played both codes until 1998. If Souths miss out in 2000 I might consider switching, but right now I want to play as many first grade games for Souths as consistently as I can.

Chapter test
1 practicing
2 past tense
3 c

CHAPTER 7: PLAY SCRIPT

Comprehension
1 c
2 Georgiou is her first grandson.
3 false
4 The Turkogolou family who own the salon are Turkish Cypriots by birth.
5 c
6 their friendship
7 b, e
8 c
9 b

Writing skills
1 b
2 a, e
3 b
4 She has been speaking before but it is only now that the audience can hear her.
5 actor movement, actor's manner of speaking,
6 so the audience can see what Penny is being shown
7 throwing the symbols into the pond
8 climax
9 God, how I hate those fish!
10 a

Focus on punctuation
1 'What's the budget for this documentary?' the producer asked.
2 'We're looking for an actor to play the dying pioneer,' said the casting director.
3 'If you can't be available for six months, you can't audition,' Peter announced.
4 The director shouted, 'Everyone on set immediately!'
5 'Where is the shield to go with this sword?' the props manager asked.
6 'Hey, Jack!' the cameraman called. 'Look to the camera, please.'

Note: Single or double inverted commas may be used.

Select a word
1 set
2 script
3 playwright
4 role
5 theatre
6 cinema

Grammar
1 **a** were going
b were getting dearer, were getting dearer, was
c are planning
d will be going
2 **a** was staging
b will be holding
c is going
d was being demolished

Word study
1 **a** practice
b direction
c skill
d illuminated
2 **a** practise
b direct
c rehearse
d instruct
3 **a** craft
b illuminate
c instruction
4 **a** editor
b scriptwriter
c director
d producer
e cameraman

Evaluating other people's writing
2, 3, 5

Word usage
1 **a** practises
b except
c principal
d illegible
2 **a** did
b might have
c could have
d should have
3 **a** might have
b off
c have fallen
d broken
e hung

Quick think
1 c
2 **a** audition
b costume
c sound effects
d producer
e director

Proofreading
'William Shakespeare wrote plays in the sixteenth century,' the teacher told his class. 'He wrote comedies, tragedies and history plays.'
'Was he an Australian?' Vincent wanted to know.
'No, he was an Englishman,' replied Mr Theodosiou.
Note: Single or double inverted commas may be used.

Idiom
1 Paul thought it was an impossible task.
2 Nguyen wanted his brother to stop talking.

Chapter test
1 instructions
2 He was climbing the old walnut tree.
3 d

CHAPTER 8: BOOK JACKET

Comprehension

1 You make it happen
2 John Marsden, Roman Stolz
3 Pan Macmillan Australia
4 $12.01
5 International Standard Book Number
6 The book is about horror and the supernatural. The illustrations and text both contain images of horror and the supernatural.
7 The reader must make choices in the plot to influence its outcome.
8 This permits identification when the book is shelved.

Writing skills

1 The word *Creep* and the chaotic print suggest horror and disorder.
2 a, d, e
3 running open-mouthed figure, hair on end
4 headstones, highlighted phrases, darkness
5 to suggest death
6 to involve the would-be reader
7 a
8 following you, no
9 the publisher

Focus on punctuation

1 Have you seen 'Happy Feet' yet?
2 It was Queen Marie Antoinette who said of the starving citizens of Paris 'Why don't they eat cake?'
3 'Play School' is a popular Australian TV production for preschoolers.
4 Our Maths teacher's favourite saying is 'See what fun algebra can be'.
5 Australian sayings such as 'flat out like a lizard drinking' are old-fashioned now.
6 'If a job's worth doing it's worth doing well,' his father told him.

Select a word

1 **a** spectre
b poltergeist
c spirit
d phantom
2 **a** fright
b terror
c dread
d panic

Grammar

1 **a** will need
b will be taking
c will be
d will have read
e will have seen
2 **a** will go
b will be
3 **a** will have gone
b should have done
4 **a** will be swimming
b will be going
c will be playing
5 **a** past continuous tense
b future tense
c future continuous tense
d future tense

Word study

1 **a** supernatural
b panic
c terror
d horror
2 **a** title
b style
c blurb
d layout
3 **a** a giant, slimy eel
b an avenging dragon
c an ogre
4 **a** difficult
b stern
c illegible
d disruptive
5 **a** Bight
b might
c plight
d flight
e tight
f edible
g possible
h sensible
i visible
j legible

Word usage

1 **a** bizarre
b gallant
2 **a** barren
b pioneers
c craters
d tunnelling
e duel
f regain
g bride
3 **a** evil
b devoured
c giant
4 Thar, noble son of the assassinated Prince of Kor, has to fight a duel with the Earl of Ido to regain his principality and his bride.

Quick think

1 **a** suicide
b homicide
c fratricide
d infanticide
e genocide
2 *~cide*
3 c, g
4 transparent, invisible

Proofreading

The driver of the red car caused the accident. He drove at high speed down the hill and through the traffic lights and collided with the old man's vehicle coming on his right.

Idiom

1 He did not understand maths at all.
2 This is meant to prove that all hens are white. In fact, it is an idiomatic expression that is completely illogical.

Writing paragraphs and whole texts

4 **a** own life story written by oneself
b life story of someone else
c an imaginary story
d a daily record of a ship's activities
e a diary, a daily record of thoughts and activities

Chapter test

1 b
2 will be
3 d

CHAPTER 9: INSTRUCTIONS

Comprehension

1 false
2 the cutting tooth
3 c
4 to cut tube length
5 d
6 to force air through sound holes
7 c
8 c

Writing skills

1 b
2 so they can be checked off as found
3 false
4 cut, insert
5 **a** stiff
b gaps
c precisely
d match
6 chronological order of performance
7 stopping
8 a, b, e
9 one after the other
10 a, b, d, e, g

Focus on punctuation

1 **a** won't
b couldn't
c wouldn't
d could've
e might've
f should've
2 **a** It's, I'll
b can't
c you're, won't
d Jim'll
e Where's
3 I wouldn't have minded if he'd asked me. He could've borrowed all my gear and it wouldn't have worried me a bit. But to take it without asking, that's too much. It's plain bad manners, as far as I'm concerned.
4 might've, could've, couldn't, wouldn't

Select a word

1 capitulate
2 visualise
3 improvise
4 estimate
5 orchestrate
6 minimise

Grammar

1 **a** have
b was
c are
d are
e is
2 **a** raced
b will compete
c swallowed
d have eaten
e laps (is lapping)
f tuned
g is lazing
h is
i swirl
j is

Word study

1 **a** harmonise
b capitulate
c improvise
d estimate
e visualise
f minimise
g orchestrate
h manipulate
i prevaricate
i analyse
2 **a** large (big)
b narrow
c plain
d night
e evergreen
f stale
g poor
h lazy
3 **a** unusual
b antimatter
c unsympathetic
d unimaginative
e anticlimax
f uninterested
g unrealistic
h antibiotic

Word usage

1 **a** wrapped around the pole
  b It, the red car, the sporty one
  c even if he saw the truck, which I don't think he did
2 **a** a red sports car
  b at high speed
3 **a** traffic light intersection
  b truck on the right
  c driver killed

Quick think

1 **a** i
  b ii
  c ii
2 **a** picture
  b sin
  c button
  d wink
  e rake
3 clichés

Proofreading

Fairy tales about the likes of Jack and his pail of water can be read in any child's story book. You can also read biblical stories like that of the baby Moses floating in his reed basket among the reeds of the Nile River.

Idiom

1 I do not like this; I would not like to have it.
2 Kai thinks he is hard done by. He wants the teacher to stop handing out homework.

Writing paragraphs and whole texts

1 c, b, d, e, f, a
2 1 Wrap kitten in blanket and keep warm.
  2 Feed 2-hourly day and night.
  3 Formula and bottle are available from vet.
  4 Wipe rear end with warm, damp cloth after feeds to encourage excretion.
  5 After kitten's eyes open, supervise play.
  6 Increase quantity and variety of food with age.
  7 Bottle-feeding is not necessary after 5 weeks.
3 I wish I were taller.

Chapter test

1 c
2 are
3 is
4 c

CHAPTER 10: FACTUAL DESCRIPTION

Comprehension

1 b
2 They jump or they chase people.
3 **a** ambushed
  b invertebrates
4 true
5 tools
6 c
7 do not
8 c
9 false

Writing skills

1 d
2 b
3 first paragraph
4 At the slightest provocation she rears to attack.
5 The speed is unusual and unexpected.
6 b
7 c
8 The funnel-web is mentioned in the title and in all three paragraphs.
9 c
10 a

Focus on punctuation

1 Carly's, Freeth's, Lear's, Bradman's
2 Marcus's, Remedios's, Petronas's
3 officers', cows', classes'
4 cattle's, fish's, people's
5 **a** A barrister's assistant is a junior counsel.
  b A dog is man's best friend.
  c The fleet's catch was stolen.
  d Peter swapped his ball for John's, John swapped that for Fred's and Mick didn't want anyone's ball.
6 **a** X
  b X
  c X
7 false

Select a word

1	inform	2	argue
3	define	4	describe
5	argue	6	manageable

Grammar

1 **a** nineteen, wild
  b old, faded, old-fashioned
  c full, empty, recycling
2 **a** excitable, unpredictable
  b additional, gentle, glistening
3 **a** the boy at the surf carnival
  b the three-year-old
  c land of music and poetry
4 **a** iii
  b i
  c ii
5 Surf lifesavers, volunteers all of them, spend their free time patrolling popular beaches to ensure no one gets swept out by an unpredictable rip or slips into deep water when a sandbar collapses

Word study

1 **a** record
  b describe
  c inform
  d outline
  e argue
  f define

2 **a** record
b argue
c define
d describe
3 **a** pharmaceutical
b manageable
c antivenene
d invertebrate

Word usage

1 **a** 9
b spat
c iii
d 4 lines
2 **a** ruthless
b loathing
c lane-way
d vaulting
3 **a** leapt
b stream
c lightly built
d dared

Quick think

1 tornado
2 gale
3 breeze
4 zephyr
5 gust
6 typhoon

Proofreading

'Be careful,' Paul's father warned him as he set off with his mates to camp in the Royal National Park. 'It's January and the funnel-webs are about.'
Paul grinned. 'They won't bite us, Dad. We're too big to ambush.'
'Don't laugh, son. The funnel-web's bite is fatal if you don't receive antivenene in time.'
Note: Single or double inverted commas may be used.

Idiom

1 John does not want to do anything new or different.
2 You do not have the skills or understanding to handle this situation.

Writing paragraphs and whole texts

a d, b, a, c, e, f

Chapter test

1 irritating
2 a large pink pig
3 c

CHAPTER 11: ADVERTISEMENT

Comprehension

1 b
2 a
3 goalkeeper
4 at night
5 for the Olympics
6 Newsagents sell tickets or they are available by ringing 03 9292 1234.
7 false
8 The question 'Can the Aussies defy the odds?' suggests that Australia is not certain of victory.
9 world class program, world class soccer match

Writing skills

1 b
2 Bosnich's recommendation will help sell programs because he is famous.
3 c
4 world
5 to attract attention with a suggestion of excitement
6 be on your toes, be at his best
7 a, c
8 a, c, f
9 The black dots mark five reasons for buying this program and each is to be found inside the program.
10 balance
11 b

Focus on punctuation

1 **a** students'
b dogs'
c parents'
d book's
2 **a** Martina inherited both her sisters' clothes but Eva's fitted her best.
b Ming Lee's father's business is doing better than many of their friends' businesses.
c Little Paul's illness was so contagious it soon became everyone's.
d The lions' roar as they went hunting set every creature's teeth on edge.
e Most nocturnal animals' eyes are round like the barn owl's eyes.
3 **a** Peter borrowed his brother John's compass and two friends' camping gear.
b He confiscated all the spies' infra-red goggles.
c A buffalo herd's hooves could be heard thundering across the plain
d The pride's cubs slept in the sun beside their lioness mothers.

Select a word

1 fame
2 admiration
3 notoriety
4 renown
5 decadence
6 ruthlessness

Grammar

1 uglier
larger
tall, tallest
longer, longest

2 dependable, most dependable
reliable, more reliable
more trustworthy, most trustworthy
malicious, most malicious
honest, more honest
3 less nervous
least famous
careful
less anxious, least anxious
less dangerous
4 **a** older
b younger
c most frightened
d sillier
e least worried

Word study
1 **a** legendary
b notorious
c renowned
d famous
2 **a** despicable
b ruthless
c decadent
d abominable
3 **a** notorious
b despicable
c legendary
4 **a** abominable
b ruthless
c decadent

Word usage
1 **a** renovated, neglected
b **i** ornate
ii sweeping
iii loaded with potential
iv a little elbow grease
v bay window
vi period style
2 **a** false
b true
c false

Quick think
1 **a** tender loving care
b as soon as possible
c or nearest offer
d after hours
2 **a** a car
b a house
c a dog
3 **a** iii
b not expect

Proofreading
Soccer's my favourite sport and I want to play with the Socceroos when I'm older. My ambition is to match Pele's record. His fame is almost legendary among soccer players.

Idiom
1 Work harder and use some energy.
2 You must make a stand on this issue, for one side or the other.

Writing paragraphs and whole texts
1 **d** Morry's Motors
b Stocktake sale
a Heaps of bargains
i All makes and models
c Be quick
f Drive away today
h Finance available
e 433 Paramatta Road
g Auburn

Chapter test
1 d
2 crankiest
3 most placid
4 b

CHAPTER 12: SPORTS ARTICLE

Comprehension
1 b
2 true
3 d
4 fluency, continuity
5 Gridiron is too slow.
6 Yes. The whole tone of the article is critical.
7 b

Writing skills
1 When the going gets tough, the tough get going.
2 a, c
3 tough take a break
4 Big American footballers coming to Australia
5 b
6 the same DNA as small apartment buildings
7 jargon
8 c
9 repetition
10 b
11 light and flippant
12 d

Focus on punctuation
1 in-struc-tion, pro-duc-tion, ab-so-lute-ly
2 **a** Australians sometimes think of Americans as baggy-trousered, cap-wearing baseball fanatics.
b Americans probably consider Australians as sausage-sizzling, Vegemite-loving cricket fanatics.
3 **a** Rihanna, Katy Perry and Kesha—they're the female voices of this decade.
b 'Modern music—can't hear a word they're singing,' muttered the old man.
c Whatever's out there—and I can't hear it now—is obviously stalking us.

4 **a** check-shirted
b transmitter-fitted
c multi-award winning
d mag-wheeled

Select a word

1	molecular	**2**	cellular
3	Polar	**4**	consular
5	angular	**6**	nuclear

Grammar

1 **a** his, them
b its
c your, his
d our
e Their
f I, he
2 **a** She invited him and all his friends over for a video veg-out night.
b He has lost a valuable watch and its case.
c He thought they stopped play too often.
d They watched him shoot six goals in a row.
e She found the family's lost dog without its identity tag.
3 **a** their
b its
c our
d she
e their

Word study

1 **a** jovial (or jocular)
b benign
c humorous
2 **a** malicious
b sarcastic
c acerbic
3 **a** biased
b jovial
c malicious
d acerbic
4 **a** malefactor
b malnourished
c malady
d malodorous
e malevolent
f malformation
g malediction
h malpractice

Word usage

1 goal attack, defending champions, shooting
2 The Thunderbirds reached/had the same score as the Ravens.
3 **a** foil
b line-out
c corner
d par
e heptathlon
4 **a** defending, victory
b attacking
c battle lines, fray

5 **a** electrical trades
b weather reporting
c goldsmithing
d surgery
e seismology

Quick think

1 – c, **2** – a, **3** – b, **4** – d, **5** – e

Proofreading

Last Wednesday's game against Duck Creek saw our boys maintain their winning streak. Behind at half-time, they came back to score three tries and clear two goals to even the score with five minutes still to go. A great run down the field from Smithy saw the ball passed to Johnno, across to Daley and straight into the arms of the man with the fastest feet in Hays Park, Charlie Singh. Charlie's try was converted by Papadopoulos and once again Hays Park had come out on top.

Idiom

1 The Kookaburras scored consecutive wins against the Koels and Rosellas this season.
2 That result is so close the winner is not immediately obvious.

Writing paragraphs and whole texts

1 **a** Y **b** i
2 [Walmer has been …
['This will be …

Chapter test

1 its
2 b
3 a
4 c

CHAPTER 13: SONG LYRIC

Comprehension

1 c
2 c
3 adults
4 the war between the generations as there is always a new generation to fight it
5 b
6 the adults who call him/her *brat*
7 Yes. The singer does not want to be seen as *the enemy*. He/she is not the enemy but is just caught in the generation gap.

Writing skills

1 b
2 d
3 first line
4 a
5 *We don't refer to the past when showing what we've done*
6 b
7 reason why the singer is called a *brat*, explanation of why he/she is not a *brat*
8 b

9 The singer is asking adults to have patience.
10 The song explains that youth are not, in fact, brats, but simply caught in the social phenomenon of the generation gap.

Focus on punctuation

1 As per your order: one set of guitar strings, two plectrums and three intermediate level score sheets.
2 List the band members by instrument: trumpeters, saxophonists, clarinet players, a flautist and a bassoonist.
3 Priest: Do you have any last words to say, Ned?
Ned Kelly: Such is life.
4 The order of procession into the hall will be as follows: Year 7, Year 8 and Year 10, in that order.
5 Here's the list of camping equipment needed: a two-man tent, a tomahawk, a frying pan and saucepan, a box of matches and a can of insect spray.
6 Don't feed the wildlife: no biscuits, lollies, cakes, fruit, meats or any other foods.
7 His last instructions: proceeds of the estate to be passed to the Foundation for Lost Dogs.
8 Interviewer: Why did you take up playing the bassoon?

Select a word

1 society
2 enemy
3 harmony
4 melody
5 arrangement
6 harmony

Grammar

1 **a** whom
b that
c whose
d which
2 **a** Kristen, who is my friend, has moved to another school.
b I delivered a pizza to Mr Jones, who is my old neighbour.
c We hired a strobe light, which was brilliant, for the disco.
d Michael went looking for the dog, which had slipped its chain and escaped.
3 **a** who
b whose
c that
d which

Word study

1 **a** ballad
b lyric
c arrangement
d harmony
e melody
2 a and b synchronise
3 **a** melodious
b harmonious
c lyrical
d societal
4 **a** harmonise
b arrange
c generate
d emerge
5 **a** emergency
b generation
c arrangement
d harmony

Word usage

1 **a** culture
b struggle
c prospect
d meagre
e disenchanted
f phenomenon
g impatient
2 **a** impatient
b meagre
c culture
d phenomenon
e disenchanted
3 **a** audition, concert
b thumped, blared, fanfare
c tune, discordant
d conducting, challenging
e insistent, attraction

Quick think

1 **a** boom
b tinkle
c trill
d clash
2 **a** strumming
b playing
c plucked
d blew
3 **a** bow
b reed
c plectrum
d pedal

Proofreading

Unless your music is what the public wants to hear your skill will take you nowhere. Aspiring stars must be prepared to play gigs in places they do not like and for money they consider paltry.

However, there is always the chance that one day a recording studio agent will hear your music in some seedy hall and offer a contract, exposure, promotion and stardom. When that happens you'll start a rollercoaster ride that will either make you a celebrity or a one hit wonder who'll be back strumming in those dingy halls inside two years.

Idiom

1 She did not fit in socially with those at the Festival.
2 Like a flash of gold in a prospecting pan his fame was very brief.

Writing paragraphs and whole texts

2 rum, inside, hair.

Chapter test
1 b
2 a
3 b

CHAPTER 14: POEM

Comprehension
1 c
2 true
3 b
4 false
5 It is sitting in the fork of a fallen tree.
6 *like a frail wisp of smoke*
7 This refers to the passing of day into night.
8 It is unknown to the poet watching the heron.

Writing skills
1 c
2 *glides, silk*
3 *hulking, death*
4 *legs like two silk banners*
5 A slim, graceful, pale grey bird.
6 *an egg, death*
7 alliteration
8 **a** 's'
b alliteration
9 c
10 a, b

Focus on punctuation
1 Oscar is very talented: he sings, he dances, he juggles.
2 The game plan was simple: run on to win, play hard to win, end up winning.
3 It was a strict regimen the crew followed: one man on watch, one man asleep, one man preparing the next meal, one man baling, and every two hours each rotated to the next post.
4 In the school Ag. Plot we run a variety of stock: lowliner cattle, suffolk ewes, fat lambs and vealers.
5 My father's pockets were filled with foreign coins: francs, marks, ringgits, yen and rupiah.
6 Regulations governing the use of the park: no dogs, no fires, no littering and no alcohol.
7 Harry's shopping list was long: nails, screws, nuts and bolts, a pair of pliers, screwdrivers and a spanner.
8 Elizabeth considered her options: walk comfortably and be late or ride her bike uphill in the heat just to be on time.

Select a word
1 fragility
2 agility
3 sleekness
4 slenderness
5 frailty
6 weakness

Grammar
1 **a** very
b quietly
c relentlessly
d least

2 **a** patiently, stylishly
b (pointlessly)
c proudly, (exceptionally)

3 **a** true **b** true
c false **d** false

Word study
1 **a** Dandelions danced
b The snake slid slowly and silently over the step
c Forty-five firemen fought the ferocious
d A series of silly slogans
2 **a** visible
b days
c voyage
d invisible
3 **a** cheerless
b disallow
c unnecessary
d unknown
e graceless
f disordered
4 **a** i, iii, vi
b **i** frail
ii fragile
iii brittle
iv weak
5 **a** unhappy
b miscued
c unfurred
d unreliable
e disagreeable
f unread

Evaluating other people's writing
1 run, track, flurry
2 **a** i, iii, iv
b i, ii, iii, v
c comma
d rhythm

Word usage
1 **a** a bull in a china shop
b a snake in the grass
c a cat among the pigeons
2 **a** a cat among the pigeons
b a bull in a china shop
c a snake in the grass
3 face
4 a
5 **a** hissed
b clinked
c howling
d chimed
e growled

Quick think

1 **a** as proud as a peacock
  b as happy as a pig in mud
  c as sly as a fox
  d as brave as a lion
2 **a** Croesus
  b Hades
  c Hercules
  d Attila the Hun

Idiom

1 This man had two impossible options. He could stay on the ship or jump into the sea. Either way he would drown.
2 Something unpleasant spoils something pleasant.

Writing paragraphs and whole texts

1 **a** e.g. as aggressive as a last quarter scrum
  b e.g. like Christmas beetles to light
  c e.g. as round and silver as a new coin
4 **a** cat
  b clapped

Chapter test

1 a
2 pinged
3 alliteration
4 much
5 b

CHAPTER 15: TELEVISION REVIEW

Comprehension

1 Video cameras, television networks
2 b
3 b
4 false
5 No, voice-overs
6 refers to *grainy videos* from various US states
7 *dross, compost*
8 c
9 b

Writing skills

1 channel, and time slot reference
2 *hand-held spy machines*
3 c
4 shark
5 They will take and show anything just as sharks will eat anything.
6 *hollers*
7 b
8 b
9 *grainy, muddy*
10 *Knowledge is power* but knowledge of the sort of show this is gives her a headache.
11 No. Sutton concentrates on all the bad points and uses exaggerated and colourful language to do so, without positive consideration of any aspect of the program.

Focus on punctuation

1 **a** Was John Curtin Prime Minister during the Second World War?
  b Dr John Flynn established the Flying Doctor Service in the Outback.
  c 'I won! I won!' he shouted, waving his lottery ticket.
2 **a** Julio, Bruno and Ben were all driven by Bruno's father.
  b I borrowed your 'Human Nature' CD—sorry, I forgot to ask for the loan of it.
  c I beat Mick's dog to the corner in two minutes flat—Mick's still getting there.

Note: In questions 1 and 2 single or double inverted commas may be used.

3 **a** The following dignitaries were present: the Mayor, the Town Clerk, the local clergy and Mr Kwong, a well-known and respected philanthropist.
  b He ate his meal quickly; he had a train to catch.

Select a word

1 belly
2 supplies
3 filly
4 miseries
5 ally
6 enemies

Grammar

1 **a** later
  b ago
  c sometimes
  d never
2 **a** everywhere
  b nowhere
  c anywhere
  d below
3 **a** anywhere
  b occasionally
  c there
  d Sometimes

Evaluating other people's writing

1 a, b, c, d, e, f
2 c
3 a, b
4 a, e, g
5 caught, cooperate
6 **a** and stuff
  b and things like that
  c I mean

Word study

1 **a** whispered
  b thunder
  c delicious
  d melodious
  e shrieked
2 **a** enthusiasm
  b rabid
  c surpass

3 **a** surpass
b rabid
c enthusiasm
d shrieked
e melodious
f delicious
4 **a** melodious
b shrieked
c delicious
d rabid
e whispered
f enthusiasm

Evaluating other people's writing

Punctuation: It's boring—she is stupid. And who wants to lookn like her anyway? None of my friends look like that.
two homonyms: reel (real), their (they're)
irrelevant statement: she is stupid
poor adjective: stupid
poor start to a sentence: I think the way that …
repetition: real like in real life
2 b, c, d, e, f

Word usage

1 **a** there
b They're
c there, there
d We're
e Where
f were
2 **a** trudged
b amble
c limped
d shuffled
e stride
3 **a** large
b gigantic
c enormous
d colossal
4 **a** microscopic
b small
c tiny
d minute

Quick think

1 **a** irksome
b dross/compost
c rabid
d coiffure
e footage
2 **a** hypermart
b hyper-hysteria
c hypercritical
d hypertension
e hyperactive
3 **a** microscope
b micromanager
c microcosm
d micro-organism
e microbat

Idiom

1 The work in this class is too difficult for me; I cannot understand it.
2 This is a colloquial expression for being very happy (as in a fire stoked up and blazing brightly).

Writing paragraphs and whole texts

1 **a** – v, **b** – vi, **c** – viii, **d** – x, **e** – i, **f** – ii, **g** – iii, **h** – ix, **i** – vii, **j** – iv
2 **a** Starring
b base
c screen
d followers
e *The Man from Snowy River*
f series
g pleased
h often
i early
j star
k ratings
l producer
m risk
n reception
o unknown

Chapter test

1 never
2 true
3 supplies
4 delicious
5 We're

Acknowledgements

The author and publisher would like to thank the following copyright holders for their permission to reprint.
Page 2, cartoon no. 4697 from *Footrot Flats* 25 reprinted by permission of Murray Ball and Diogenes Designs Ltd; p. 8, cartoon on greenhouse gas reprinted by permission of Jon Kudelka; p. 9, extract from *Black Belt* by Nicole Plüss reprinted by permission of the copyright owner, c/- Curtis Brown (Aust); p. 32, extract from *Moxiana* by Michael Stephens reprinted by permission of HarperCollins; p. 40, interview of Samantha Riley by Anthony Raineri reprinted by permission of *Total Sports*; p. 55, cover of book *Creep Street* by John Marsden reprinted by permission of Pan Macmillan Australia; p. 70, article titled 'Milking funnel-webs' by Karen McGhee reprinted by permission of *Australian Geographic*; p. 77, photo of Mark Bosnich reprinted by permission of Getty Images; p. 74, extract from *Murder at the City Wall* by Xu Ning reprinted by permission of Kevin Baker; p. 85, article titled 'When going gets tough, tough take a break' reprinted by permission of Ray Chesterton; p. 93, lyrics for The Living End song 'Prisoner of Society' reprinted by permission of Rae Harvey; p. 100, poem titled 'The Heron' by Nicolette Stasko reprinted by permission of Curtis Brown (Aust); p. 108, review titled 'World's wildest police videos' by Gerri Sutton reprinted by permission of *Who Weekly*.

Efforts have been made to gain permission for all copyright material reproduced in this book, but we have not been successful in contacting all copyright holders. If you are one of these people, please contact Pascal Press.

NOTES

NOTES